W9-CSQ-171

Summer SPLASH

LEARNING ACTIVITIES

Brighter Child®
An imprint of Carson-Dellosa Publishing LLC
Greensboro, North Carolina

Brighter Child®
An imprint of Carson-Dellosa Publishing LLC
P.O. Box 35665
Greensboro, NC 27425 USA

ISBN 978-1-60996-970-7

01-051121151

Table of Contents

Making the Most of
Summer Splash Learning Activities

This resource contains a myriad of fun and challenging reading and math activities. The reading pages provide practice in reading for details, compare and contrast, analogies, and similes and metaphors. The math pages review skills taught in third grade, such as multiplication and division, fractions and decimals, and problem solving.

Most of the activities in the book are designed so that your child can work independently. However, your child will enjoy the activities much more if you work alongside him or her. Make sure to let your child know that this is not a workbook with tests, but a book of fun activities that you can do together. The book is divided into 10 weeks, with about eight activity pages per week. Feel free to choose how many per day and in which order you do the activities, but complete the weeks in sequence, since activities become increasingly challenging as the book progresses.

Summer Splash Learning Activities provides an important link between your child's third- and fourth-grade school years. It reviews what your child learned in third grade, providing the confidence and skills that he or she needs for the coming fall. The activities in this book will help your child successfully bridge the gap between third and fourth grade by reviewing and reinforcing the important and essential skills for his or her continued academic success. These activities are designed to

- review skills in math, reading, and language arts that your child learned the previous year.

- give you an opportunity to monitor your child's skills in various areas.

- offer you a chance to spend special time with your child.

- enable your child to continue routine daily learning activities.

- give you a chance to praise your child's efforts.

- demonstrate to your child that you value lifetime learning.

- make you an active and important part of your child's educational development.

Getting Started

In order for your child to get the most from the activities in this resource, use these helpful tips to make these learning experiences interesting and, most of all, fun!

- Set aside a time each day for completing the activities. Make it a time when your child will be most ready to learn, and make it a routine.

- Provide a pleasant, quiet place to work. This means no TV in your child's work area. Also, make sure there is a sufficient light source.

- Review in advance the activity page(s) your child will complete that session. This way, you will be able to familiarize yourself with the lesson.

- Have your child read the directions aloud beforehand to make sure he or she understands the activity. Instructions are written for the child, but he or she may need your help reading and/or understanding them.

- Let your child help choose which activity he or she would like to complete that day.

- Praise all your child's work. It's the effort, not necessarily the end result, that counts most.

No one knows better than you how your child learns best, so use this book to enhance the way you already work with him or her. Use every opportunity possible as a learning experience, whether making a trip through the grocery store or riding in the car. Pose problems and let your child figure out how to solve them, asking questions such as *Which route should we take to the park? What could we use to make a plant grow straight?* or *How high should we hang this shelf?* Also, respond excitedly to discoveries your child makes throughout the day with comments such as *That rock is really unique! I wonder how long it took the spider to spin that web;* or *You spent your money wisely.* In this way, you will encourage and motivate your child to learn throughout the day and for the rest of his or her life, providing the confidence and self-esteem he or she needs for continued academic success.

Everyday Learning Activities

Use these simple educational activities to keep your child's mind engaged and active during the summer months and all year long!

- Ask your child to make a schedule of events for the day, in the order in which they will take place. Ask him or her to prioritize the list and number the events.

- On a neighborhood walk or while driving in the car, encourage your child to read all the street signs and numbers.

- Read with your child each day. Encourage your child to retell the story to you. Then, have him or her make up original adventures for the story characters or write an additional chapter.

- Have your child write down important dates such as family birthdays, important trips or outings, or holidays. Be sure your child capitalizes the name of the month and week and uses a comma between the day and year.

- During a visit to the park or playground, invite your child to describe what he or she sees there, using as many adjectives as possible.

- Have your child list three things you can smell, feel, taste, or see in a particular room of the house or on a "senses walk."

- Have your child identify as many parts of the human body as he or she can. Ask him or her to describe the function of each part, if possible.

- Ask your child to read a recipe with you for a simple dish. Practice measuring skills by simulating measuring out the ingredients with water or rice in measuring spoons or cups.

- Have your child read the price of items in a store or supermarket. Challenge him or her to estimate how much can be bought with a designated amount of money. Can your child figure out how much change is left over?

- Encourage your child to tell you whether certain objects in your home (sofa, pencil) would be measured in pounds or ounces.

- Fill a measuring cup with water to different levels, and invite your child to read the measurement and then write it as a fraction.

- Encourage your child to read nonfiction library books and make up creative stories about the subject matter (e.g., lions or airplanes).

6

Assessment

Read the passage and answer questions 1–9.

Choosing a Pet

Choosing the right pet is not simple. You cannot just fly by the seat of your pants, because the decision that you make will have lasting consequences for you, your family, and the pet you choose. Before choosing a pet, you must consider many things.

First, decide whether you are ready for the daily responsibility of caring for another life. It will be up to you to make sure that your pet is well cared for, even if you are tired, sick, or have other things to do. Also, consider the amount of free time that you will have each day to spend with your pet. Dogs need to be walked and played with every day. A lizard does not require as much care—especially the walking part!

If you think that you are ready to take care of a pet, consider how you want to spend time with it. Do you think that it would be fun to have a playful pet, like a dog, or would you be happier with a pet that is quieter, such as a hamster, fish, or bird?

Next, think about the size of pet that could live comfortably in your home. Do you have a yard? Some animals need room to run outside, while other pets can live quite happily in the house.

Finally, visit your local animal shelter before heading to the pet store. You will find a variety of animals there that need loving homes. Your next pet might be at a shelter waiting to share your home, your love, and your life!

1. Underline the sentence that tells the main idea.

2. List three supporting details.

_____

_____

_____

3. Write a synonym of *simple*. _____

4. Write an antonym of *sick*. _____

5. Write a homophone of *need*. _____

6. Write a simile about a happy pet. _____

_____

7

Assessment

7. Circle the idiom located in the first paragraph.

8. Complete the analogy. Kitten is to cat as _____ is to dog.

9. Why do you think the author wrote the passage "Choosing a Pet"?

   A. to entertain readers with interesting stories about pets

   B. to inform readers about the things they should consider when choosing a pet

   C. to persuade readers to adopt homeless pets

10. Using the Venn Diagram below, compare and contrast two types of pets.

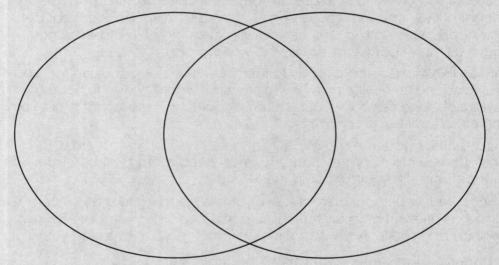

11. Read the following sentences. Write *O* if the sentence is an opinion. Write *F* if it is a fact.

_____ Cats are better pets than dogs.

_____ Pets need responsible care.

_____ Everyone should have a pet.

_____ All animals make good pets.

12. On another sheet of paper, write a story from a puppy's point of view about the child who is adopting it.

Assessment

Read the passage and answer questions 13–17.

Marcy's Bike

Marcy rode her new bike to Danielle's house. Danielle and Marcy took turns riding the new bike. They each rode it around the block several times. Marcy showed Danielle how she could ride her bike without holding on to the handlebars. Danielle wanted to try, too. Danielle started riding and shouted, "Look, no hands!" Then, Danielle fell on the sidewalk. She stood up right away. Marcy asked if she was all right. Danielle said, "I'm fine, but I think your handlebars are twisted."

13. Which of the following events happens second?

    A. Danielle falls on the sidewalk.

    B. Marcy rides her new bike to Danielle's house.

    C. The girls take turns riding Marcy's new bike.

14. Who are the main characters in the story? _____

    Where does the story take place? _____

    What is the problem in the story? _____

    _____

15. How do the handlebars become bent? _____

16. What do you think will happen next? _____

    _____

17. Read the following sentences. Write *C* beside the sentence that states the cause. Write *E* beside the sentence that states the effect.

    _____ The handlebars on Marcy's new bike become bent.

    _____ Danielle loses her balance and falls off Marcy's bike.

Assessment Analysis

Answer Key:

1. Choosing the right pet is not simple.
2. Decide whether you are ready for the daily responsibility of caring for a pet. Consider how much time you want to spend with your pet. What size of pet could live comfortably in your home?
3. easy
4. well
5. knead, kneed
6. Answers will vary.
7. fly by the seat of your pants
8. puppy
9. B
10. Answers will vary.
11. O, F, O, O
12. Stories will vary.
13. C
14. Marcy and Danielle, Danielle's neighborhood, Danielle falls off Marcy's new bike and bends the handlebars.
15. Danielle falls off the bike.
16. Answers will vary.
17. E, C

After reviewing the assessment, match the problems answered incorrectly to the corresponding activity pages. Your child should spend extra time on those activities to strengthen his or her reading skills.

Number	Skill	Activity Page(s)
1.	main idea	14–17
2.	reading for details	22–25
3., 4.	synonyms and antonyms	38–39
5.	homophones	30
6.	similes and metaphors	31–32
7.	idioms	33
8.	analogies	40–41
9.	author's purpose	46–47
10.	compare and contrast	48–49
11.	fact or opinion	54–55
12.	point of view	56–57
13.	sequencing	62–65
14.	character analysis	70–71
15.	drawing conclusions	78–81
16.	predicting outcomes	72–73
17.	cause and effect	86–88

Assessment

Write each number in the correct column.

1. Even	10	Odd	2. Even	6	Odd
_____	21	_____	_____	9	_____
_____	39	_____	_____	18	_____
_____	42	_____	_____	27	_____
	72			88	
	91			95	

Write each number in expanded form.

3. 3,242 _____

4. 743 _____

5. 10,806 _____

Write > or < to compare the numbers.

6. 465 ◯ 312   193 ◯ 198   17 ◯ 20

7. $\frac{1}{5}$ ◯ $\frac{1}{2}$ 0.4 ◯ 0.2   1,000 ◯ 999

Use the underlined digit to round to the greatest place value.

8. 5$\underline{7}$ = _____   4$\underline{8}$1 = _____   5$\underline{0}$2 = _____

Solve each problem.

9.
```
  3,208        $8.72        325,202        1,631
+ 2,603        + 0.65       + 43,119       + 800
```

10.
```
   593         7,649          600         $18.05
 -  76        - 3,202        - 219        - 1.32
```

Assessment

Solve each problem.

11.
$$424 \times 19$$
$$\$0.87 \times 22$$
$$3\overline{)680}$$
$$22\overline{)1,804}$$

12.

What time is it? _____

What time will it be in 40 minutes? _____

What time was it 3 hours and 5 minutes earlier? _____

13. Jon has a 1-dollar bill, 4 quarters, 1 dime, 2 nickels, and 3 pennies in his pocket. What is the total amount of money that Jon has in his pocket?

_____

Reduce to lowest terms.

14.
$$\frac{4}{8} = \underline{\hspace{1cm}}$$
$$\frac{6}{36} = \underline{\hspace{1cm}}$$
$$\frac{5}{25} = \underline{\hspace{1cm}}$$
$$\frac{11}{2} = \underline{\hspace{1cm}}$$

Find the perimeter.

15. 8 ft.

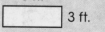 3 ft.

P = _____ ft.

Find the area.

16. 7 cm

 6 cm

A = _____ sq. cm

Find the volume.

17.

2 yd.   4 yd.   6 yd.

V = _____ cu. yd.

Solve.

18. Michael's class read 37 books one week, 43 books the next week, and 28 books the week after that. How many books did Michael's class read in all?

_____ books

Assessment Analysis

Answer Key:

1. Even: 10, 42, 72;
   Odd: 21, 39, 91
2. Even: 6, 18, 88;
   Odd: 9, 27, 95
3. 3,000 + 200 + 40 + 2
4. 700 + 40 + 3
5. 10,000 + 0 + 800 + 0 + 6

6. >, <, <
7. <, >, >
8. 60, 500, 500
9. 5,811; $9.37;
   368,321; 2,431
10. 517; 4,447; 381,
    $16.73

11. 8,056; $19.14, 226 r2, 82
12. 8:00, 8:40, 4:55
13. $2.23
14. $\frac{1}{2}$, $\frac{1}{6}$, $\frac{1}{5}$, $5\frac{1}{2}$
15. 22
16. 42
17. 48
18. 108 books

After reviewing the assessment, match the problems answered incorrectly to the corresponding activity pages. Your child should spend extra time on those activities to strengthen his or her math skills.

Number	Skill	Activity Page(s)
1., 2., 3., 4., 5., 6., 7., 8.	numeration	18–21
9., 10.	addition and subtraction	26–29
11.	multiplication and division	34–37, 42–45
12., 13.	time and money	50–53
14.	fractions and decimals	58–61, 66–69
15., 16., 17.	geometry	74–77, 81–84
18.	problem solving	89–92

Primates

> The **main idea** tells what a passage is mostly about. The main idea in a paragraph is often stated in the first or second sentence and may be summed up in the final sentence.

Read the paragraphs. Underline the sentence in each paragraph that tells its main idea.

One reason to classify animals is to determine which are related to each other. Usually, such classification is achieved by studying the skeletons and skins of the animals. Have you ever wondered to which animals you are related?

Monkeys and apes belong to a group called *primates*. (The word *primate* comes from a Latin word that means "first.") Monkeys and apes are called primates because they have complex brains. They are the most intelligent of all animals. Human beings are also classified as primates. Monkeys and apes have large brains like we do, and they use the ends of their front limbs as hands. Monkeys, apes, and humans can think and use tools.

One type of primate, the chimpanzee, eats mostly fruits. However, it also will eat vegetables. It has even been seen eating insects and small animals. Chimpanzees use sticks to get honey from a honeycomb or to dig ants and termites from their nests.

What's in a Name?

Read each paragraph. Then, circle the letter next to the sentence that gives the main idea.

1. Amber Wilson hated her name. Without even trying, she could think of 20 better names. In fact, when her family moved to Lakeville, she thought about telling everybody that her name was Madison. She decided that it wasn't a good idea. She might not turn around when someone said, "Madison." She hated the name *Amber*, but she was used to it.

   A. Amber thought of 20 other names.

   B. Amber Wilson hated her name.

2. Then, Amber read a chapter about gems in her science book. She learned that pieces of amber were fossils, like dinosaur bones. They started out as sap. Trees with layers of sap on their trunks aged and died. When they fell down, they were covered with dirt or water. The trees were buried for millions of years, and lumps of dry, hard sap became amber.

   A. Amber comes from sap.

   B. Trees were buried.

3. She found out that some pieces of amber have bugs or parts of plants in them. Long ago, in a prehistoric forest, insects landed on the sticky sap. They couldn't get away. Another layer of sap oozed down on top of them. It preserved them. Some of those bugs were alive during the age of dinosaurs.

   A. Insects were covered by sap.

   B. Some pieces of amber have bugs or parts of plants in them.

Extra! Everyone in Amber's class read the chapter. They all wanted to be named after a gem, especially one with bugs inside from the age of dinosaurs. Do you like your name? Why or why not?

_____

_____

Insects

Read the passage. Underline the sentence in each paragraph that tells the main idea.

Insects are truly amazing animals. They come in beautiful colors and a variety of interesting shapes. Insects are almost everywhere! They live in cold and hot climates. They live in wet jungles and dry deserts. They can live underground and high in the trees. There are at least one million different species of insects, and every year, new species are discovered.

Insects do many of the same things that humans do, but they do them in unique ways. Insects can hear, but some insects hear with hairs that cover their bodies. Other insects have hearing organs on their legs or hear from the sides of their bodies. Some insects smell with their antennae. Others taste with their feet.

Some insects are beneficial to humans. Bees make honey. Bees, wasps, butterflies, and other insects pollinate flowers and other plants. Some fruits and vegetables would not produce seeds if bees, wasps, butterflies, and other insects did not pollinate them. Some insects eat or destroy pests that ruin our crops. Insects are also an important part of many animals' diets. Birds, fish, and frogs eat insects. Some insects even taste good to people!

Some insects are harmful to humans. There are insects that eat crops. Other insects get into our homes and destroy our clothes, books, and stored foods. Termites can be serious pests when they chew the wood frames of buildings! Worst of all, some insects carry diseases that can make people very sick.

Although all insects have six legs, three body parts, and two antennae, each species of insects is unique. Insects can be beautiful or ugly, helpful or harmful, or noisy or quiet. With all of that variety, insects help make the world a very interesting place.

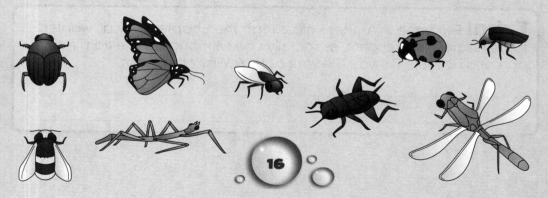

16

Aesop's Fables

Usually, the main idea in a story or passage is stated at the beginning. There are times when it is stated at the end. Aesop's Fables are examples of this. They tell stories to illustrate lessons or morals. The ends of the stories usually wrap up or summarize the lessons.

Read the synopsis of each fable. Circle the letter next to the moral that summarizes each story.

The Hare and the Tortoise

One day, a hare was making fun of a tortoise and called him a slowpoke. That made the tortoise mad, so he challenged the hare to a race. Of course, the hare knew that he would win. When the hare was far enough ahead, he stopped for a rest and fell asleep. The tortoise plodded along, never stopping. When the hare woke up, he ran as fast as he could to the finish line. However, the tortoise had already crossed it. The moral of the story is . . .

1. **A.** a lazy hare is fast.
   B. do not brag or boast.
   C. the slow turtle wins.

The Fox and the Crow

A crow sat in a tree with a piece of cheese that she had just taken from an open window. A fox who was walking by saw the crow and wanted the cheese. The fox complimented the crow in many ways. The fox told the crow how nicely she sang. To prove her voice, the crow opened her mouth to sing. The cheese fell out, and the fox gobbled it up. The moral of the story is . . .

2. **A.** do not let flattery go to your head.
   B. listen before you sing.
   C. eat fast so that you will not lose your dinner.

17

Ordering Numbers

To find the order of numbers, compare their **place value** columns. Order from greatest to least:

The same numeral is in the hundreds, so move to the tens.

347 (3)

268 (4)—The least because it has a 2 in the hundreds place.

363 (2)—The second greatest because its tens place is bigger.

1,619 (1)—The greatest because it has 4 digits.

Study the example above. Then, write the numbers in order from greatest to least.

1.

172	905	730	340

_____, _____, _____, _____

2.

1,170	2,314	800	512

_____, _____, _____, _____

3.

982	4,000	960	6,000

_____, _____, _____, _____

4.

401	472	436	490

_____, _____, _____, _____

greatest — 2nd greatest — 3rd greatest — least

Write the numbers in order from least to greatest.

5.

87	107	71	17

_____, _____, _____, _____

6.

96	906	600	19

_____, _____, _____, _____

7.

1,900	2,700	7,000	4,350

_____, _____, _____, _____

8.

620	6,200	200	2,600

_____, _____, _____, _____

Writing in Expanded Form

The place value system is based on groups of ten. This chart shows how the **ones, tens, hundreds,** and **thousands** relate to each other.

1,000	100	10	1
1 thousand = 10 hundreds	1 hundred = 10 tens	1 ten = 10 ones	one

This chart is helpful when writing numbers in expanded form. **Example:** 3,649 = 3,000 + 600 + 40 + 9

Study the example above. Then, write each number in expanded form.

		1,000	100	10	1
1.	9,516 =	+	+	+	
2.	2,358 =	+	+	+	
3.	1,407 =	+	+	+	
4.	921 =	+	+	+	
5.	7,800 =	+	+	+	
6.	3,264 =	+	+	+	
7.	5,182 =	+	+	+	
8.	614 =	+	+	+	
9.	4,073 =	+	+	+	
10.	9,530 =	+	+	+	

Comparing Numbers

The **greater than (>)** and **less than (<)** symbols always point to the number of lesser value. Numbers of equal value use the equal sign (=).

Examples: 543 > 53   24 < 359   204 = 204

Study the examples above. Then, use the symbols >, <, and = to compare each pair of numbers.

1.   61 ◯ 60   4,128 ◯ 2,199   2,145 ◯ 8,415

2.   34 ◯ 43   542 ◯ 249   809 ◯ 809

3.   24 ◯ 14   1,215 ◯ 5,187   9,214 ◯ 4,482

4.   351 ◯ 350   51,215 ◯ 51,215   814 ◯ 4,285

5.   921 ◯ 9,219   319,114 ◯ 312,546   312 ◯ 645

6.   48 ◯ 48   5,198 ◯ 426   8,249 ◯ 511

7.   92 ◯ 28   3,291 ◯ 5,982

8.   432 ◯ 396   5,214 ◯ 6,294

Compare the year you were born with these numbers: 1,815; 1,995; 2,075.

20

Rounding

When **rounding** a number, always look to the digit to the right of the place to which you are rounding. If that digit is 4 or less, round down. If it is 5 or more, round up.

Examples: Nearest ten: 34   Nearest hundred: 487   Nearest thousand 2,279
34: round down to 30   487: round up to 500   2,279: round down to 2,000

Study the examples above. Then, solve each problem.

Round to the nearest ten.

1. 72 _____   14 _____

2. 83 _____   49 _____

3. 55 _____   62 _____

4. 17 _____   29 _____

5. 34 _____   95 _____

6. 68 _____   41 _____

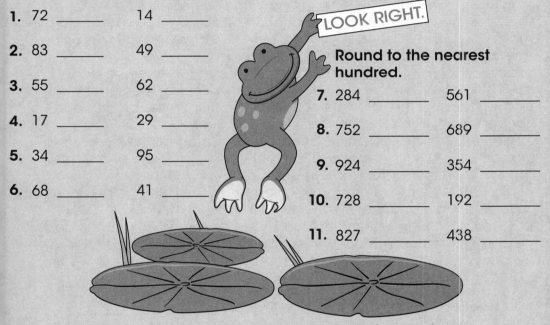

LOOK RIGHT.

Round to the nearest hundred.

7. 284 _____   561 _____

8. 752 _____   689 _____

9. 924 _____   354 _____

10. 728 _____   192 _____

11. 827 _____   438 _____

Use the underlined digit to round to the greatest place value.

12. 2<u>1</u>,432 _____   7<u>2</u>,418 _____   5<u>8</u>1,242 _____

13. 4,<u>2</u>99 _____   6,<u>4</u>19 _____   7,<u>5</u>46 _____

14. 9,<u>7</u>21 _____   4,<u>1</u>42 _____   5,<u>9</u>48 _____

15. 3<u>8</u>,201 _____   3<u>4</u>,112 _____   6,<u>4</u>18,205 _____

Mike and Moe

An author includes many **details** to help the reader better understand a story. Details provide the reader with a clearer picture of the story elements, such as characters, setting, and plot.

Read the story and answer the questions.

We chose our first cat, Mike, at the animal shelter when he was only eight weeks old. He is white with orange stripes.

When Mike was about two years old, I heard a faint cry while I was reading on the patio. I looked around in the shrubbery, under the furniture, and on the brick wall around the patio, but I did not see a thing. The crying persisted. Finally, about three feet above where I was sitting, I saw a tiny kitten hanging from a tree branch.

I called for my brother, Ben, to bring a ladder. Together, we leaned it against the tree. I held the ladder while Ben climbed up the first two rungs and reached for the kitten. Ben gently pulled it from the branch and handed me the tiniest kitten that I had ever seen.

We took the kitten to our veterinarian. She said that the kitten was probably about four weeks old. She told us how to feed him a special formula with an eyedropper. Ben and I fed the kitten this way for two weeks before he could drink from a saucer. As the kitten gained weight, he looked more and more like Mike. We named him Moe.

At first, Mike was not nice to Moe. Then, he learned to ignore Moe. Now, they are good friends. Moe is half of Mike's size and is scared of his own shadow. We have no idea how Moe ended up in that tree, but we are glad that he did. We think Mike is, too.

1. How high did Ben climb on the ladder? _____

2. When did Moe come to the house? _____

3. How many places were searched before Moe was found? _____

4. How long did Moe have to be fed with a dropper? _____

5. What was the author doing when he heard Moe's cry? _____

6. Where did the author's family get Mike? _____

22

Traffic Rules

You probably already know many traffic rules. Review the traffic rules. Then, use them to answer the following questions.

- Never run into the street. Stop at the curb or by the edge of the road.
- Always look left, right, and left again before crossing the street. Check to see if a vehicle is coming around the corner.
- Use your ears as well as your eyes. If you hear sirens, move out of the path of traffic immediately.
- Obey all traffic signs and signals. Do not speed up to cross during a yellow light.
- Cross on crosswalks or at corners.
- Never cross between parked cars.
- Watch out for cars backing out of driveways.
- Do not play in the street or in parking lots.
- Walk on sidewalks whenever they are available. If there are no sidewalks, walk on the left side of the road facing traffic.
- When crossing a street, walk quickly. Do not run, because you could fall. Do not walk slowly, because a vehicle that was not there when you last looked may be coming.
- If you have to walk through busy traffic areas, plan your route ahead of time.
- If you have to walk outside after dark, carry a flashlight and wear bright, colorful clothing.

1. What should you do before crossing a street? _____

   _____

2. What are three ways not to cross a street?_____

   _____

3. Where is the best place to cross a street?_____

   _____

4. What should you do when you are walking outside at night?_____

   _____

5. If there are no sidewalks, where should you walk?_____

   _____

The Saguaro Cactus

Read the passage.

In the Arizona desert, there is a cactus that will live 100 years or more. The saguaro cactus grows very slowly in the hot, dry desert, and it becomes home to many animals as it grows.

The cactus starts as a seed that is dropped from the fruit of a mature saguaro cactus. The seed sprouts after receiving moisture from a rare rain. The seed swells up, splits its shell, and sends a root into the desert soil. The seed sends up a stem that is green, moist, and covered with prickles.

It does not rain often in the desert, so the stem grows slowly. During its first year, it grows less than 0.39 inches (1 cm). After 10 years, it may be only 6 inches (15 cm) tall. When it is 50 years old, the original stem is about 15 feet (4.5 m) high. After 50 years, the saguaro cactus grows its first branches. The branches are moist and prickly, like the trunk. Over the next 50 years, the cactus may grow as tall as 35 feet (10.5 m).

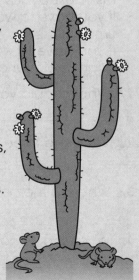

Many animals make their homes in saguaro cacti. They like the moist skin of the cacti. A woodpecker may build a deep nest in the side of a saguaro stem and lay its eggs there. After the eggs hatch, the baby birds eat insects that live on the cactus. Mice, hawks, and owls may also use the nest built by the woodpecker.

Beautiful flowers grow on the mature saguaro cactus. The flowers provide juicy nectar for birds, insects, and bats.

After the flowers dry up, green fruit covers the cactus. The fruit is sweet and juicy. Many animals come to eat the fruit. They spread the seeds from the fruit onto the ground, where the seeds wait for rain. Eventually, these seeds will sprout and grow new saguaro cacti.

The Saguaro Cactus

Draw the stages of the saguaro cactus life cycle. Label the pictures using the words in the box.

50 years   flowers   seed sprouts   animal homes   fruit   100 years

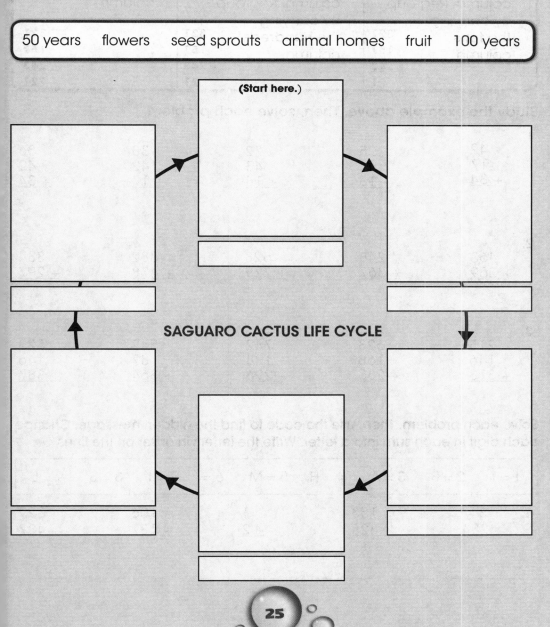

(Start here.)

SAGUARO CACTUS LIFE CYCLE

Column Addition Riddle

1. Add the **ones** column. Regroup by carrying the **tens** column.	2. Add the **tens** column. Regroup by carrying the **hundreds** column.	3. Add the **hundreds** column.
¹ 321 157 + 243 = 1	¹¹ 321 157 + 243 = 21	¹¹ 321 157 + 243 = 721

Study the example above. Then, solve each problem.

1.

| 42 17 + 34 | 25 43 + 18 | 72 43 + 18 | 38 42 + 17 | 56 42 + 34 |

2.

| 463 + 259 | 248 + 367 | 528 + 279 | 382 + 478 | 384 + 297 |

3.

| 215 146 + 318 | 623 168 + 235 | 742 128 + 296 | 542 187 + 364 | 523 146 + 387 |

Solve each problem. Then, use the code to find the hidden message. Change each digit in each sum into a letter. Write the letters in order on the lines.

1 = T	2 = B	3 = A	4 = H	5 = M	6 = !	7 = I	8 = S	9 = L

4.

| 247 + 284 | 153 + 325 | 1 + 2 | 106 + 187 | 329 + 487 |

___ ___ ___ ___   ___ ___ ___   ___ ___ ___ ___

Mixed Practice Number Puzzle

Fill in the number puzzle using the clues provided.

Across

1. 2,000 + 500 + 30 + 5
2. 550,000 + 420 + 30
3. 7,800 − 2,000 − 400 − 50
4. 70,000 + 6,000 + 470 + 2
5. 19,165 + 120 + 5
6. 6,985 − 1,550 − 3,000 − 35
7. 49,915 − 22,000 − 610
8. 5,000 + 32,000 + 400 + 96

Down

4. 50,000 + 22,000 + 395 + 5
9. 30,000 + 8,000 + 200 + 25
10. 15,448 − 7,200 − 7,100 − 2
11. 50,475 − 15,000 − 200 − 50
12. 55,000 + 275 + 25 + 30
13. 13,565 − 9,000 − 300 − 45
14. 82,690 − 40,000 − 1,000 − 420
15. 77,200 − 5,000 − 100 − 10

27

Adding and Subtracting Money

When adding and subtracting money, the **decimal point** must line up in the problem and in the sum or difference. Then, you can add or subtract. Remember to include the dollar sign ($) in your answer.

$$\begin{array}{r} \$3.42 \\ +\ 1.25 \\ \hline \$4.67 \end{array} \qquad \begin{array}{r} \$2.58 \\ +\ 1.23 \\ \hline \$3.81 \end{array} \qquad \begin{array}{r} \$13.42 \\ +\ 2.81 \\ \hline \$16.23 \end{array}$$

Study the examples above. Then, solve each problem.

1.
$$\begin{array}{r} \$\ 0.51 \\ +\ 0.92 \\ \hline \end{array} \qquad \begin{array}{r} \$3.45 \\ +\ 4.82 \\ \hline \end{array} \qquad \begin{array}{r} \$41.23 \\ +\ 29.38 \\ \hline \end{array} \qquad \begin{array}{r} \$0.94 \\ -\ 0.38 \\ \hline \end{array}$$

2.
$$\begin{array}{r} \$2.75 \\ -\ 1.82 \\ \hline \end{array} \qquad \begin{array}{r} \$38.41 \\ -\ 19.24 \\ \hline \end{array} \qquad \begin{array}{r} \$423.14 \\ +\ 180.93 \\ \hline \end{array} \qquad \begin{array}{r} \$525.42 \\ +\ 48.29 \\ \hline \end{array}$$

3.
$$\begin{array}{r} \$42.91 \\ +\ 318.09 \\ \hline \end{array} \qquad \begin{array}{r} \$301.24 \\ -\ 130.19 \\ \hline \end{array} \qquad \begin{array}{r} \$421.24 \\ -\ 150.82 \\ \hline \end{array} \qquad \begin{array}{r} \$500.27 \\ -\ 123.16 \\ \hline \end{array}$$

Solve each problem. Then, use the code and write the letters in order on the blanks to find out what Jeremis bought with the money he saved.

1 = E	6 = B
2 = N	7 = W
3 = Y	8 = C
4 = A	9 = I
5 = L	0 = !

4.
$$\begin{array}{r} \$91.70 \\ -49.53 \\ \hline \end{array} \qquad \begin{array}{r} \$80.90 \\ -11.07 \\ \hline \end{array} \qquad \begin{array}{r} \$86.15 \\ -\ 1.05 \\ \hline \end{array}$$

___ ___ ___

___ ___ ___ ___ ___ ___

Using Parentheses

Always complete the operation inside of the parentheses first. Then, solve.

Example: $(18 - 10) + 7 = \square \longrightarrow 18 - 10 = 8 \longrightarrow 8 + 7 = \boxed{15}$

Study the example above. Then, solve each equation.

1. $(4 + 5) + 7 = \underline{\hspace{2cm}}$ $7 + (4 + 5) = \underline{\hspace{2cm}}$

2. $17 - (3 + 5) = \underline{\hspace{2cm}}$ $11 - (2 + 3) = \underline{\hspace{2cm}}$

3. $(7 + 7) - 8 = \underline{\hspace{2cm}}$ $13 - (3 + 5) = \underline{\hspace{2cm}}$

4. $(4 + 6) - 7 = \underline{\hspace{2cm}}$ $(6 + 3) + 8 = \underline{\hspace{2cm}}$

5. $(18 - 7) + 4 = \underline{\hspace{2cm}}$ $(6 + 7) - 6 = \underline{\hspace{2cm}}$

6. $5 + (3 + 5) = \underline{\hspace{2cm}}$ $(15 - 7) + 9 = \underline{\hspace{2cm}}$

7. $(16 - 7) + 4 = \underline{\hspace{2cm}}$ $7 + (10 - 2) = \underline{\hspace{2cm}}$

8. $(14 - 9) + 7 = \underline{\hspace{2cm}}$ $8 + (6 + 3) = \underline{\hspace{2cm}}$

9. $7 + (14 - 6) = \underline{\hspace{2cm}}$ $(17 - 9) + 4 = \underline{\hspace{2cm}}$

10. $(3 + 3) + 8 = \underline{\hspace{2cm}}$ $(20 - 10) + 5 = \underline{\hspace{2cm}}$

11. $(17 - 8) + 7 = \underline{\hspace{2cm}}$ $(4 + 8) - 7 = \underline{\hspace{2cm}}$

12. $5 + (15 - 8) = \underline{\hspace{2cm}}$ $13 - (4 + 3) = \underline{\hspace{2cm}}$

29

It Sounds the Same

> **Homophones** are words that are pronounced the same but are spelled differently and have different meanings.
>
> **Example:** Mom went *to* the meeting at school. Dad went, *too*. The *two* of them met my teacher.

Complete the following sentences by circling the correct homophone. Then, on a separate sheet of paper, write a sentence using the other homophone.

1.   The (bough, bow) of the tree hung low over the sidewalk.

2.   Liz had been sick for four days and was (board, bored) with staying in bed.

3.   The wranglers watched the (heard, herd) on the range.

4.   Ben and Alex went (threw, through) the passage that led into the cave.

5.   An (ark, arc) is a type of boat.

6.   In (witch, which) shop did you find your new shoes?

7.   Dad stopped and asked for the (way, weigh) to the stadium.

8.   The camper put a (great, grate) over the fire and boiled water on it.

Nonsense Words

There is a nonsense word in each pair of sentences below. Read each sentence. Then, write a word on the line that makes sense in place of the nonsense word in both sentences.

1. Isabel and Brett rode their bikes to the *flibber* down the street.

We watched Gretchen *flibber* the car in the driveway.

The nonsense word *flibber* means _____.

2. The little, white dog is Tyrone's new *prackle*.
Would you like to *prackle* this cat?
The nonsense word *prackle* means _____.

3. My mom asked me to *tirth* the baby to sleep.
When we were on the beach, I found a beautiful *tirth* with a fossil leaf imprint.
The nonsense word *tirth* means _____.

4. Do not step on the *blape* in the sidewalk!

While making breakfast, I can *blape* the eggs on the pan.

The nonsense word *blape* means _____.

5. I cannot chew gum, because it will *verg* to my braces.

My dad asked me to pick up every *verg* in the yard.

The nonsense word *verg* means _____.

6. I can tell time on my new *jeffa*.

Will you *jeffa* me at my swim meet?

The nonsense word *jeffa* means _____.

Comparing Two Things

A **metaphor** is a comparison of two unlike things. It does not use the comparison words that are found in similes.

Example: The moon was a lamp lighting up the night.

Circle the two words being compared in each sentence. Then, write how the two words are alike or what it is about them that is being compared.

1. The row of trees are soldiers standing at attention.

   _____

2. From the airplane, the cars below were ants crawling along the highway.

   _____

3. The circus clowns were sardines packed in one car.

   _____

4. The sound of waves lapping the shore reminded me of dogs slopping water.

   _____

5. The fans' stamping feet in the bleachers were drums beating inside my head.

   _____

It's a Figure of Speech

An **idiom** is a figure of speech. Often, it is a phrase. It says one thing and means another.

Circle the letter next to the correct meaning of the italicized idiom in each sentence.

1. He is *a big cheese* at the high school.
   A. a cafeteria worker   **B.** the principal   **C.** a very important person

2. When I met the doctor, she gave me a *dead fish* handshake.
   A. limp   **B.** strong   **C.** wet

3. Tommy would *give you the shirt off his back* if necessary.
   A. lend you his shirt   **B.** help you any way he could   **C.** keep you warm

4. She did not talk about her family, because she did not want to reveal *the skeletons in her closet.*
   A. her family secrets   **B.** where she kept the trash   **C.** the end of a scary story

5. My mom is *the top dog* at the office.
   A. the loudest one   **B.** the one in charge; the boss   **C.** the office supplier

6. Let us *bury the hatchet* and get on with our lives.
   A. forget the past   **B.** stop chopping trees   **C.** go to the movies

7. The kid who always hides my books is a real *thorn in my side.*
   A. prickly plant   **B.** bothersome person   **C.** ticklish person

8. I really *put my foot in my mouth* when I offered to bake all of the cakes for the bake sale.
   A. spoke before thinking   **B.** hurt my mouth   **C.** was angry

9. The kid with the whiny voice is not *my cup of tea.*
   A. making the right tea   **B.** my kind of person   **C.** friendly to me

33

Understanding Multiplication

The answer to a multiplication problem is called the **product.** The numbers being multiplied are called **factors.**

To **multiply** means to use repeated addition. It is easier to understand if you imagine equal groups, then add all of the groups together.

It looks like this:

$4 + 4 + 4$
3 groups of 4
3×4 ← factors
12 ← product

Study the example above. Then, write an addition and a multiplication problem for each picture. Find the sum and the product.

1.
✕✕✕✕✕
✕✕✕✕✕
✕✕✕✕✕

☐ + ☐ + ☐ = ☐
☐ ✕ ☐ = ☐

2.
☆ ☆ ☆
☆ ☆ ☆

☐ + ☐ = ☐
☐ ✕ ☐ = ☐

3.
●● ●●
●● ●●

☐ + ☐ + ☐ + ☐ = ☐
☐ ✕ ☐ = ☐

4.
ⓔ ⓔ ⓔ ⓔ
ⓔ ⓔ ⓔ ⓔ

☐ + ☐ = ☐
☐ ✕ ☐ = ☐

5.
✕ ✕ ✕
✕ ✕ ✕
✕ ✕ ✕

☐ + ☐ + ☐ = ☐
☐ ✕ ☐ = ☐

6.
★★★★
★★★★
★★★★

☐ + ☐ + ☐ = ☐
☐ ✕ ☐ = ☐

7.
●●
●●
●●

☐ + ☐ + ☐ = ☐
☐ ✕ ☐ = ☐

8.
ⓔ ⓔ ⓔ ⓔ ⓔ
ⓔ ⓔ ⓔ ⓔ ⓔ

☐ + ☐ = ☐
☐ ✕ ☐ = ☐

34

Multiplying with Two-Digit Factors

1. Multiply the ones.	3**2** x **4** **8**	2. Multiply the bottom factor in the ones column with the top factor in the tens column.	**3**2 x **4** **128**

Study the example above. Then, find each product.

1.
94
x 2

63
x 3

80
x 8

42
x 3

2.
61
x 9

72
x 2

91
x 7

52
x 4

3.
73
x 3

60
x 6

53
x 2

71
x 5

4.
92
x 4

21
x 9

91
x 8

82
x 2

Multiplying with Regrouping

1. Multiply the ones. Regroup if needed.	2. Multiply the tens. Add the extra tens. Regroup if needed.	3. Multiply the hundreds. Add the extra hundreds.
$\overset{2}{2}65$ x 5 5	$\overset{3\,2}{2}65$ x 5 25	$\overset{3\,2}{2}65$ x 5 1,325

Study the example above. Then, find each product.

1.
364	378	354	671
x 2	x 2	x 3	x 4

2.
500	534	439	266
x 3	x 8	x 2	x 5

3.
180	911	236	741
x 5	x 9	x 3	x 3

4.
372	407	165	290
x 4	x 2	x 7	x 6

Multiplying Larger Numbers

1. Multiply the ones.	2. Place a zero in the ones column. Multiply by the tens digit.	3. Add.
3 3 **378** x **34** **1512**	2 2 3 3 **378** x **34** 1512 **+11340**	2 2 3 3 3̸78 x 34 1512 + 11340 **129852**

Study the example above. Then, find each product.

1.
    310   412   362   420
x 24   x 35   x 28   x 41

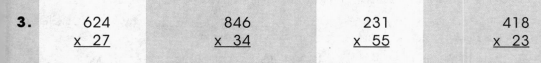

2.
    543   246   185   324
x 23   x 51   x 43   x 81

3.
    624   846   231   418
x 27   x 34   x 55   x 23

It Means the Same

A **synonym** is a word that has the same or nearly the same meaning as another word. A synonym may be used in place of another word while not changing the meaning of the sentence.

Examples: The man carried all of his money in a brown *sack*. The man carried all of his money in a brown *bag*. The man carried all of his money in a brown *pouch*.

Choose a synonym from the box for each italicized word. Write the word on the line following its italicized synonym.

required	plans	constructed	pupils	finished
trip	place	country	sprinkling	welcomed

1. The fourth-grade students were going on a two-day *journey* _____ to learn more about their state's history.

2. Everyone was excited about the trip and knew that good *arrangements* _____ must be made in order to have a successful adventure.

3. When planning, they considered the weather, *necessary* _____ clothing, and how much money they would need.

4. The day that the trip began, it was *drizzling* _____ in the morning.

5. But, that did not bother the *students* _____, because each had brought a raincoat.

6. The bus traveled through one *rural* _____ town after another until it reached the State History Museum.

7. Once inside, they were *greeted* _____ by Ms. Handler, a guide, who took them through the museum.

8. The students learned that the state's capitol had been *built* _____ many years ago.

9. After the guide *completed* _____ the tour, the students thanked her and left to continue their trip.

10. Before heading to the next *stop* _____, the students ate the lunches that they had prepared before leaving home that morning.

Opposite Meanings

An **antonym** is a word that has the opposite meaning of another word.

Example: The *little* dog played with its new toy. The *big* dog played with its new toy.

Unscramble each of the following words. The underlined letter is the first letter of each unscrambled word. Select a word from the box that is the antonym for the unscrambled word. Then, write it on the line next to the unscrambled word.

prompt	increase	find	calm	treasure
exaggerate	refuse	enormous	question	tense

	Scrambled Word	Unscrambled Word	Antonym
1.	ypol<u>d</u>wan		
2.	l<u>a</u>low		
3.	so<u>l</u>e		
4.	tmo<u>s</u>ry		
5.	snerw<u>a</u>		
6.	<u>t</u>nyi		
7.	r<u>t</u>yda		
8.	axe<u>r</u>lde		
9.	hs<u>t</u>ar		
10.	eu<u>r</u>edc		

Extra! On another sheet of paper, write the words to your favorite song. Then, replace several of the words with their antonyms. How does this change the song?

What's the Similarity?

> An **analogy** is a comparison or relationship between two or more things that may otherwise not be alike. To complete an analogy, first determine what the relationship between the words is. Then, determine what word could be added to keep the relationship the same.

Write the word from the box that completes each analogy.

1. Subtraction is to _____ as division is to multiplication.

2. Anchor is to ship as brake is to _____.

3. Humidity is to _____ as arid is to desert.

4. _____ is to tracks as bus is to road.

5. _____ is to river as dolphin is to ocean.

6. Deep is to _____ as high is to mountain.

7. _____ are to hands as toes are to feet.

8. Key is to door as combination is to _____.

9. Sapphire is to _____ as emerald is to green.

10. Aisle is to _____ as path is to woods.

11. Violin is to bow as piano is to _____.

12. Cheese is to mouse as acorn is to _____.

13. Barn is to _____ as coop is to chickens.

14. Freeze is to froze as _____ is to stood.

15. Rain is to monsoon as wind is to _____.

trout
canyon
blue
car
addition
squirrel
tornado
keys
stand
cows
safe
train
fingers
store
tropics

Do They Agree?

Read each pair of words. Circle the word that belongs in the blank.

1. Sleep is to bed as mail is to
_____.
motor   letter   nurse

2. Dim is to bright as weak is to
_____.
strong   loose   dangerous

3. Creek is to brook as _____ is to
path.
trail   garden   bridge

4. Rabbit is to bunny as _____ is to
calf.
horse   bird   cow

5. Slick is to slippery as _____ is to
fast.
swift   slow   old

6. Bed is to boy as _____ is to
baby.
feather   dentist   cradle

7. Steel is to car as _____ is to
house.
brass   wood   silver

8. Poodle is to dog as _____ is to
bird.
lion   spider   sparrow

9. Niece is to nephew as sister is
to _____.
brother   cousin   father

10. Apple is to fruit as _____ is to
vegetable.
plum   juice   corn

Understanding Division

To **divide** means to make equal groups or to share equally. The answer to a division problem is called the **quotient.** It looks like this:

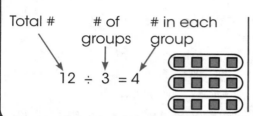

Total #   # of groups   # in each group

$12 \div 3 = 4$

Total #   # of groups   # in each group

$10 \div 2 = 5$

Study the example above. Then, circle equal groups to find the quotient.

1.

☆ ☆ ☆ ☆ ☆
☆ ☆ ☆ ☆ ☆

$10 \div 5 = \boxed{}$

2.

■ ■ ■ ■ ■
■ ■ ■ ■ ■
■ ■ ■ ■ ■

$15 \div 3 = \boxed{}$

3.

○ ○ ○
○ ○ ○

$6 \div 3 = \boxed{}$

4.

@ @ @ @
@ @ @ @

$8 \div 2 = \boxed{}$

5.

☆ ☆ ☆
☆ ☆ ☆
☆ ☆ ☆

$9 \div 3 = \boxed{}$

6.

■ ■ ■ ■
■ ■ ■ ■
■ ■ ■ ■

$12 \div 4 = \boxed{}$

7.

● ● ● ● ● ●
● ● ● ● ● ●

$12 \div 6 = \boxed{}$

8.

@ @ @ @ @ @
@ @ @ @ @ @
@ @ @ @ @ @

$18 \div 3 = \boxed{}$

9.

☆ ☆ ☆ ☆ ☆ ☆ ☆
☆ ☆ ☆ ☆ ☆ ☆ ☆

$14 \div 7 = \boxed{}$

Basic Division

Sometimes, the **dividend** is much larger than the basic facts you have learned. In these problems you will need to do more than one step to find the quotient. Use these steps to help you:

1. Does 4 x ___ = 5? No. 4) 56	2. Use the closest smaller dividend: 4 x 1 = 4 $\begin{array}{r} 1 \\ 4\overline{)56} \\ -4 \end{array}$	3. Subtract to find the remainder. Bring down the 6. $\begin{array}{r} 1 \\ 4\overline{)56} \\ -4\downarrow \\ \overline{16} \end{array}$	4. Does 4 x ___ = 16? Yes! 4 x 4 = 16 $\begin{array}{r} 14 \\ 4\overline{)56} \\ -4\downarrow \\ \overline{16} \\ -16 \\ \overline{0} \end{array}$

Study the example above. Then, divide.

1. 6) 96   2) 98   5) 90   7) 84

2. 5) 75   3) 87   8) 96   2) 76

3. 6) 84   3) 54   4) 96   5) 85

43

Division with Remainders

Sometimes, when you try to make equal groups, there are numbers left over. They are called **remainders.** Use these steps to find remainders:

Find
4)18

4 groups of 4 = 16
2 left over = r2
So . . . 4 r2
4)18

1. Does 4 x ___ = 18
   NO!
   Think: 4 x ___ is the closest to 18?

2. Use the closest smaller dividend:
   4 x 4 = 16

$$\begin{array}{r} 4 \\ 4\overline{)18} \\ -16 \\ \hline 2 \end{array}$$

3. Subtract to find the remainder. The remainder is always less than the divisor.

$$\begin{array}{r} 4\ r2 \\ 4\overline{)18} \\ -16 \\ \hline 2 \end{array}$$

Study the example above. Then, find each quotient and its remainder.

1.   8)34   4)26   7)67   3)17

2.   9)29   5)42   6)47   9)83

3.   6)39   4)19   5)24   8)79

4.   7)41   6)23   9)60   4)15

Dividing by Two Digits

1. Is the hundreds digit great enough to divide into? No. Is the 13 tens great enough to divide into? No. So, you must divide into the 137 ones.

21)137

2. How many groups of 21 are there in 137? Round the divisor to 20. Think: There are five 20s in 100. There is one more in 37. So the partial quotient must be 6.

```
    5            1
20)100      20)37
-  100       -  20
    0          17
```
5 + 1 = 6

Think about rounding the divisor to predict the amount of the partial quotient.

3. Divide. Multiply and subtract. Is the difference less than the divisor? Yes. Then, go on.

```
     6
21)137
-  126
    11
```

4. Is the difference of 11 great enough to divide into? No. So, 11 becomes the remainder.

```
        6 r11
21)137
-  126
    11
```

Note: The remainder can be any amount, as long as it is less than the divisor (in this case the divisor is 21).

Study the example above. Then, divide.

1. 17)54   32)130   41)215   11)106   22)180

2. 49)190   39)244   52)436   19)80   61)500

3. 31)150   78)399   81)161   29)223   13)75

45

Taking Care of Teeth

Read the passage.

Long ago, people cleaned their teeth in interesting ways. They scratched their teeth with a stick, wiped them with a rag, or even chewed on crushed bones or shells. Tooth care has come a long way in the past few hundred years. Now, we have fluoride toothpaste, dental floss, and specially angled toothbrushes to keep our teeth healthy.

It took someone with a lot of time on his hands to invent the first toothbrush. In the 1770s, a man named William Addis was in prison. While he was wiping his teeth with a rag, he had the idea to make a tool for cleaning teeth. He used a bone and some bristles from a hairbrush. He carefully drilled holes in one end of the bone. Then, he trimmed the brush bristles and pushed them into the holes that he had drilled. He glued the bristles into place and had the first toothbrush.

People have used different tooth cleaners over the years. Many cleaners, such as crushed bones and shells, actually damaged the protective enamel on teeth. Chalk was a popular cleaner in the 1850s. Baking soda was also used for many years, because it was abrasive. Some toothpastes still contain baking soda. Other people used salt as a tooth cleaner. Many of today's toothpastes contain sodium, too. Fluoride was first added to toothpaste in 1956 and greatly reduced the number of cavities in children. Most recently, calcium was added to toothpaste in the 1960s to help strengthen teeth.

Using dental floss once a day is one of the most important things that you can do for your teeth. Originally, the thin string was made of silk. Now, dental floss comes in different colors and flavors, tape, and waxed and unwaxed varieties. Dental floss removes "interproximal plaque accumulation," which means that it scrapes off the plaque between your teeth, where a toothbrush cannot reach.

The inventions and improvements in dental care have helped people maintain stronger, healthier teeth. We now know how to care for our teeth every day.

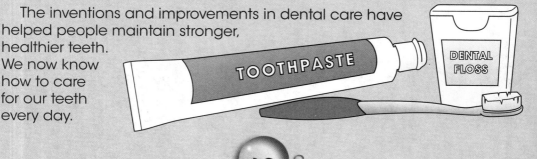

Taking Care of Teeth

Circle the letter next to the answer.

1. Why did the author write this passage?
   A. to entertain   **B.** to teach   **C.** to sell something

2. What kind of passage is "Taking Care of Teeth"?
   A. a factual passage   **B.** a humorous passage   **C.** a fictional passage

3. What is the main idea of the passage?
   A. how to take care of teeth   **B.** the importance of flossing   **C.** the history of dental care

Complete the diagram with details from the passage (page 46).

The Importance of Dental Floss
_____
_____
_____

Tooth Cleaners Over the Years
_____
_____
_____

Tooth Care

Tooth Cleaning Today
_____
_____
_____

The Invention of the Toothbrush
_____
_____
_____

The *Titanic*

The *Titanic* was one of the finest ships ever built. It was designed to be comfortable and luxurious. It was like a floating palace. Read the passage to discover what life was like on this expensive ship that made only one voyage.

There were three levels of tickets. The most expensive tickets were first class. The next level was second class. The least expensive tickets were for people traveling in third class, or steerage.

The 329 first-class passengers had four decks on which to move around. They could visit with friends in the sitting rooms of their cabins and in several different lounges, restaurants, and dining rooms. They had a gym, a pool, a Turkish bath, a library, and beautiful, sunny decks. Their meals were made from the fanciest and most expensive foods, such as mutton chops, chicken galantine, and apple meringue. Dinners consisted of many courses, and first-class passengers could choose their meals from a menu. They ate at tables decorated with china plates, crystal, and fresh flowers. Some people in first class wrote about what the ship was like. It was even fancier than what most wealthy people had at home.

The 285 second-class passengers were treated how first-class passengers on other ships were treated. Their cabins were nice, but small. They ate a four-course meal each evening at nice tables with pretty plates. Like first class passengers, they could go on deck to walk around or sit in the sun. Their decks were smaller, however, because they held the lifeboats. Second class also did not have the restaurants, gyms, and other special rooms that the first class passengers had.

The 710 third-class passengers had space in the noisy rear of the ship below second class. There were only 220 cabins in steerage. Families used these cabins. The other passengers slept in large rooms. The men slept in one room, and the women slept in another room. The steerage sitting room was a large, plain room with benches and tables. Third-class passengers had to take turns eating in a dining room that sat only 473 people at a time. Tickets told them when to eat. If they missed their times, passengers went hungry until the next meal. There were no restaurants for them.

Most of the passengers knew that they were on a special trip. The *Titanic* was supposed to be the finest ship ever built. Some very rich and famous people were on the ship for its first trip. Of course, no one on board knew that the boat would sink. This fact probably made the *Titanic*'s first and only trip across the ocean the most famous voyage of all time.

The *Titanic*

Answer the following questions using complete sentences.

1. How did meals in first class differ from meals in second class?

_____

_____

_____

2. What was in the first-class cabins that was not in the second- or third-class cabins?

_____

3. How did the sleeping rooms in third class compare to the ones in first and second class?

_____

_____

4. What did most passengers know about this trip?

_____

Read the words below of each passenger. Write *1* if the passenger who is speaking traveled first class on the *Titanic*, *2* if the passenger traveled second class, and *3* if the passenger traveled third class.

_____ "I love my room. I have a beautiful bedroom with a private sitting room."

_____ "My favorite meal is dinner, when we have a delicious four-course meal."

_____ "We swam for hours in the pool this afternoon."

_____ "In the evening, we sit on benches in the only room that we all share. We play music and dance."

_____ "I love to sit on the deck in the sun. My brother likes to play under the lifeboats."

_____ "We had a nice meal. We had to eat a little fast so that the next group of people could eat."

Telling Time to Five-Minute Intervals

The **minute hand** on a clock is the long hand. It takes 5 minutes to move from one number on the clock to the next. Therefore, we count by 5 as the minute hand moves from one number to the next. To read this clock, we say:

 20 minutes past 3:00
or
3:20

 40 minutes past 9:00
or
9:40

Study the examples above. Then, write each time two ways.

1. [ ] minutes past [ ]

[:]

2. [ ] minutes past [:]

[:]

3. [ ] minutes past [:]

[:]

4. [ ] minutes past [:]

[:]

5. [ ] minutes past [:]

[:]

6. [ ] minutes past [:]

[:]

7. [ ] minutes past [:]

[:]

8. [ ] minutes past [:]

[:]

Elapsed Time

To find out what time it will be later, add the **elapsed** time to the current time. **Example:** It is 10:42. What time will it be in 1 hour and 28 minutes? One hour later than 10:42 is 11:42. Twenty-eight minutes later than 11:42 is 12:10.

10:42

12:10

Study the example above. Then, use the clocks to answer each question.

1.

What time does the clock show? _____

What time would it be if it was 20 minutes earlier?_____

What time will it be in 3 hours and 35 minutes?_____

What time will it be in 65 minutes?_____

2.

What time does the clock show? _____

What time would it be if it was 48 minutes earlier?_____

What time will it be in 5 hours and 22 minutes?_____

What time will it be in 57 minutes?_____

3.

What time does the clock show? _____

What time would it be if it was 8 hours and 15 minutes earlier? _____

What time will it be in 4 hours and 15 minutes?_____

What time will it be in 75 minutes? _____

51

Comparing Coins

Values of money can be made using different combinations of coins. Each group of coins below is equal.

 = 25¢    = 25¢    = 25¢

Study the example above. Then, complete each equation.

1. 5 nickels = _____ quarter

2. 50 pennies = _____ dimes

3. 1 dollar = _____ quarters

4. 4 half dollars = _____ dollars

5. 10 dimes = _____ nickels

6. 2 quarters = _____ nickels

7. 50 pennies = _____ nickels

8. 3 dollars = _____ quarters

9. 6 quarters = _____ dimes

10. 2 dimes = _____ pennies

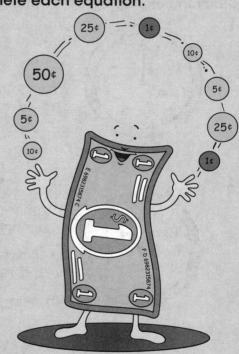

Write two ways to make each total value.

11. $2.50 = _____ or _____

12. $1.00 = _____ or _____

13. $0.75 = _____ or _____

14. $1.25 = _____ or _____

Calculating Change

Have you ever paid for something and been given change back? The cashier figures your change using these steps:

1. Begin with the amount you paid the cashier.
2. Subtract the amount you owe from the amount you paid.
3. The difference is your change.

$$\begin{array}{r} {\scriptstyle 4 \quad 9 \ 10} \\ \$\cancel{5}.\cancel{0}\cancel{0} \\ -\ 0.75 \\ \hline \$4.25 \end{array}$$

Study the example above. Then, find each amount of change that is owed to the customer.

1. Paid	$6.00	
Owe	– 2.10	

2. Paid $20.00
Owe – 16.20

3. Paid $8.00
Owe – 3.95

4. Paid $10.00
Owe – 4.60

5. Paid $9.00
Owe – 8.50

6. Paid $5.00
Owe – 0.95

7. Paid $16.00
Owe – 15.15

8. Paid $25.00
Owe – 5.00

9. Paid $2.00
Owe – 1.19

10. Paid $4.00
Owe – 3.95

That's a Fact!

Read each sentence. Circle *fact* if the statement is a fact. Circle *opinion* if the statement is an opinion.

1. When Europeans came to the land that is now the United States, there were huge flocks of swans.   Fact   Opinion

2. Hunters killed the big, white birds for their feathers.   Fact   Opinion

3. After years of being hunted, most of the swans were gone.   Fact   Opinion

4. The bird artist John James Audubon drew with a swan feather.   Fact   Opinion

5. Swan feathers were better than metal pens for drawing.   Fact   Opinion

6. It was important to save these beautiful birds.   Fact   Opinion

7. The Red Rock Lakes National Wildlife Refuge was started in Montana.   Fact   Opinion

8. The swans could not be hunted.   Fact   Opinion

9. It is wonderful that swans are coming back.   Fact   Opinion

10. A boy swan is called a *cob*, and a girl swan is called a *pen*.   Fact   Opinion

11. The calls of trumpeter swans are not very pretty.   Fact   Opinion

12. Trumpeter swans are named for the sounds that they make.   Fact   Opinion

Is That a Fact?

Read each sentence. Circle *fact* if the statement is a fact. Circle *opinion* if the statement is an opinion.

1. Eric the Red was a Viking.   Fact   Opinion

2. Vikings were brave people.   Fact   Opinion

3. Vikings lived in lands that are now Norway, Sweden, and Denmark.   Fact   Opinion

4. There was not much good farmland in the cold north.   Fact   Opinion

5. Vikings sailed to distant lands.   Fact   Opinion

6. The Vikings built great ships.   Fact   Opinion

7. Eric the Red had red hair.   Fact   Opinion

8. Eric the Red settled Greenland.   Fact   Opinion

9. Greenland is a beautiful place to live.   Fact   Opinion

10. Eric the Red's son was Leif Erikson.   Fact   Opinion

Extra! Using the keyword *Viking*, search the Internet to find out more about these daring warriors.

Chewing Gum

Read the passage.

My name is Thomas Adams. You probably have no idea who I am. I invented chewing gum. Actually, *invented* might be a strong word.

I lived in the 1800s. I once met General Santa Anna. He was a military general from Mexico. Santa Anna told me about a dried sap called *chicle*. He liked to chew this sap, which comes from the sapodilla tree. He said that Mayans and others had been chewing it for hundreds of years. I tried some. Honestly, I thought it tasted terrible.

Still, I was interested in chicle because it was so rubbery. I thought that maybe I could make things, like toys or boots, out of it. But, nothing I tried seemed to work. It would just not replace rubber.

One day, I popped a terrible-tasting piece of chicle in my mouth and chewed and chewed. "Yuck," I thought. "Wouldn't it be nice if it had some flavor?" Eureka! I had a great idea! So, I opened a flavored-gum factory and sold chewing gum like crazy.

Americans loved my gum. But, doctors seemed to think that it was bad. They said that it was bad for people's teeth. That may be true, but one doctor even said, "Chewing gum will exhaust the salivary glands and cause the intestines to stick together." Is that not the silliest thing that you have ever heard?

I am proud to say that flavored chewing gum was a hit, even though no one knows my name!

56

Chewing Gum

Circle the best answers.

1. How does the author feel about chicle?
   - **A.** friendly
   - **B.** curious
   - **C.** disgusted
   - **D.** angry

2. How does the author feel about flavored chewing gum?
   - **A.** embarrassed
   - **B.** worried
   - **C.** proud
   - **D.** curious

3. What did the author think that the chicle could do?
   - **A.** replace gum
   - **B.** become rubber
   - **C.** replace rubber
   - **D.** ruin teeth

4. What did the author think about what one doctor said?
   - **A.** He was right.
   - **B.** He was silly.
   - **C.** He was late.
   - **D.** He was smart.

Answer the questions using complete sentences.

5. Why does the author think that people should know his name?

   _____

   _____

6. Write a brief summary of the passage from your own point of view.

   _____

   _____

   _____

7. Write a brief summary of the passage from the point of view of the doctor who did not think that gum was safe.

   _____

   _____

   _____

Adding Fractions with Unlike Denominators

1. Create equivalent fractions with a common denominator.	2. Add.	3. Reduce to lowest terms.
$\dfrac{1}{8}$ $\dfrac{1\times2}{8\times2}$ $\dfrac{2}{16}$ $+\dfrac{2}{16}$ $+\dfrac{8}{10}$ $\dfrac{2}{16}$	$\dfrac{2}{16}$ $+\dfrac{2}{16}$ $\dfrac{4}{16}$	$\dfrac{4\div4}{16\div4}=\dfrac{1}{4}$

Study the example above. Then, solve each problem. Reduce if possible.

1. $\dfrac{1}{5}+\dfrac{1}{10}$ $\dfrac{1}{12}+\dfrac{4}{6}$ $\dfrac{1}{7}+\dfrac{7}{14}$

2. $\dfrac{3}{6}+\dfrac{1}{3}$ $\dfrac{1}{4}+\dfrac{5}{8}$ $\dfrac{1}{8}+\dfrac{1}{2}$

3. $\dfrac{3}{10}+\dfrac{2}{5}$ $\dfrac{1}{6}+\dfrac{5}{12}$ $\dfrac{5}{10}+\dfrac{2}{5}$

4. $\dfrac{1}{12}+\dfrac{1}{6}$ $\dfrac{3}{10}+\dfrac{1}{2}$ $\dfrac{2}{16}+\dfrac{3}{8}$

Subtracting Fractions with Unlike Denominators

1. Create equivalent fractions with a common denominator.	2. Subtract.	3. Reduce to lowest terms.
$$\frac{8}{10} \quad \frac{8}{10} \quad \frac{8}{10}$$ $$-\frac{2}{5} \quad -\frac{2 \times 2}{5 \times 2} \quad -\frac{4}{10}$$	$$\frac{8}{10}$$ $$-\frac{4}{10}$$ $$\frac{4}{10}$$	$$\frac{4 \div 2}{10 \div 2} = \frac{2}{5}$$

Study the example above. Then, solve each problem. Reduce if possible.

1.

$$\frac{3}{4} \qquad \frac{14}{16} \qquad \frac{4}{5}$$
$$-\frac{1}{2} \qquad -\frac{5}{8} \qquad -\frac{5}{10}$$

2.

$$\frac{5}{6} \qquad \frac{1}{3} \qquad \frac{2}{4}$$
$$-\frac{2}{3} \qquad -\frac{1}{12} \qquad -\frac{1}{8}$$

3.

$$\frac{7}{9} \qquad \frac{5}{6} \qquad \frac{4}{8}$$
$$-\frac{11}{18} \qquad -\frac{9}{12} \qquad -\frac{1}{2}$$

4.

$$\frac{6}{8} \qquad \frac{3}{5} \qquad \frac{13}{14}$$
$$-\frac{1}{2} \qquad -\frac{5}{10} \qquad -\frac{6}{7}$$

Finding Fractions of Whole Numbers

$\frac{1}{4}$ of 16 Divide the whole number by the denominator. $\quad$ $16 \div 4 = 4$ Multiply this quotient by the numerator. $\quad$ $1 \times 4 = 4$	$\frac{1}{4}$ of 12 $12 \div 4 = 3$ $1 \times 3 = 3$ The denominator tells us how many equal groups to make. The numerator tells us how many of these groups to add together.

Study the examples above. Then, solve each problem.

1. $\frac{1}{3}$ of 15 $\qquad$ $\frac{1}{6}$ of 12 $\qquad$ $\frac{1}{2}$ of 10 $\qquad$ $\frac{1}{4}$ of 20

   _____ $\qquad$ _____ $\qquad$ _____ $\qquad$ _____

2. $\frac{1}{7}$ of 14 $\qquad$ $\frac{1}{8}$ of 24 $\qquad$ $\frac{1}{7}$ of 28 $\qquad$ $\frac{1}{3}$ of 27

   _____ $\qquad$ _____ $\qquad$ _____ $\qquad$ _____

3. $\frac{1}{5}$ of 30 $\qquad$ $\frac{1}{8}$ of 40 $\qquad$ $\frac{1}{4}$ of 36 $\qquad$ $\frac{2}{5}$ of 10

   _____ $\qquad$ _____ $\qquad$ _____ $\qquad$ _____

4. $\frac{1}{5}$ of 45 $\qquad$ $\frac{2}{3}$ of 21 $\qquad$ $\frac{4}{6}$ of 12 $\qquad$ $\frac{1}{10}$ of 20

   _____ $\qquad$ _____ $\qquad$ _____ $\qquad$ _____

5. $\frac{1}{4}$ of 16 $\qquad$ $\frac{3}{5}$ of 15 $\qquad$ $\frac{1}{8}$ of 64 $\qquad$ $\frac{3}{4}$ of 20

   _____ $\qquad$ _____ $\qquad$ _____ $\qquad$ _____

Using Decimals

Fractions that are **tenths** ($\frac{1}{10}$) or **hundredths** ($\frac{1}{100}$) can be written as a decimal. When there are no whole numbers, put a 0 in the ones place.

$\frac{4}{10} = 0.4 =$
four tenths

$1\frac{3}{10} = 1.3 =$
one whole and
three tenths

$\frac{14}{100} = 0.14 =$
fourteen
hundredths

$1\frac{23}{100} = 1.23 =$
one whole and
twenty-three hundredths

Study the examples above. Then, write each fraction as a decimal. Color each balloon with tenths blue. Color each balloon with hundredths green.

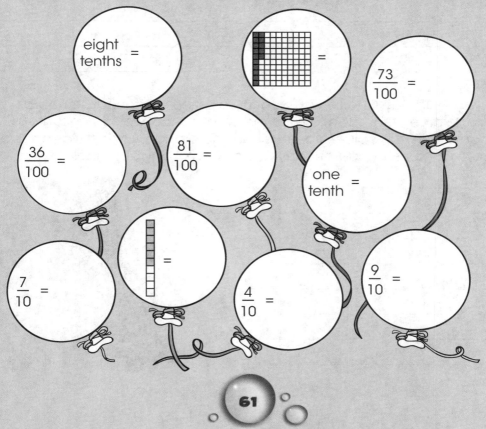

eight tenths =

=

$\frac{73}{100} =$

$\frac{36}{100} =$

$\frac{81}{100} =$

one tenth =

=

$\frac{7}{10} =$

$\frac{4}{10} =$

$\frac{9}{10} =$

Almost Late

Putting a series of events in a logical order is called **sequencing**.

The sentences in the paragraphs are out of order. Rewrite each paragraph so that it makes sense.

1. Charlie had to run to catch the school bus. If he had eaten breakfast at home, he would have had a three-mile walk to school. The alarm did not go off in the Cole house, and everyone overslept. When Charlie found a seat and sat down, he ate the apple that he had grabbed on his way out the door.

_____

_____

_____

_____

_____

2. It was Field Day. Charlie was wearing a green shirt because he was on the green team. That meant the entire school was divided into six teams: red, white, blue, green, yellow, and orange. Charlie was glad to be on the bus, because today was a special day at school.

_____

_____

_____

_____

_____

_____

Flower Pressing

The following sentences are out or order. Number the sentences in a sensible order that explains how to press flowers.

_____ Pansies, violets, small grass flowers, and petunias are the best flowers for pressing. Pick them when they are at their prettiest.

_____ Before you find flowers, make sure that you have everything else you need.

_____ Place a thick layer of newspaper over the tissue.

_____ Then, find flowers or leaves that are good for pressing.

_____ Put several heavy books on top of the newspaper.

_____ Leave the tissue, newspaper, and books this way for 24 hours.

_____ Lay the flowers flat between two layers of facial tissue.

_____ Replace the tissue and put the newspaper and books back for another 24 hours to ensure that the flowers will dry.

_____ After 24 hours, carefully remove the books, newspaper, and tissue.

Now that you know how to make pressed flowers, use them to make a floral picture. Read the mixed-up directions below and number them in a logical order.

_____ First, cut out two circles from different colors of construction paper. Make one circle a little larger than the other.

_____ Finally, put a ribbon through the hole, tie it in a loop, and hang the floral picture.

_____ With the circles ready, use tweezers to arrange the pressed flowers in a nice arrangement and glue them into place.

_____ Next, glue the small circle on top of the larger one.

_____ You will need scissors, tweezers, a paper hole punch, ribbon, white glue, construction paper, and pressed flowers.

_____ Then, punch a hole on the outer rim of the joined circles.

Emma's Job

Read the passage.

My name is Emma. I am an editor at a publishing house. My job is to find great children's stories and help them get published as books that you can buy in a store or check out at the library. I love my job. Let me tell you all about it.

Many people send me their ideas for books. Some of the ideas are not very good, some are OK, and some are great. I look for the ones that I think are great and that I think kids would love to read. If I like an author's idea, I ask her to send me a copy of her story.

Authors get ideas for stories in many ways. Some write about imaginary things. Others write about things that actually happened. Authors can tell a story just like it really happened, or they can change the events to make the story more interesting. As they write, authors try to think of the right words to tell the story. They might make lists of words, take notes, or make outlines. Sometimes, authors need more information to write. They may go to the library, take field trips, or look up their topics on the Internet. When they write, authors change words that don't sound right.

When the author is finished writing the story, she sends a copy of it to me. If I like it, I call the author and offer to publish her story. Then, I read the story again. I give the author suggestions for making the story even better. I tell the author what I really like, and I may recommend some better words. Many people read the book and offer suggestions for making it better. The author rewrites the story until it is just right.

When the book is finished, I work with a designer to plan how the book will look. We choose the size of the book, the font, and the style of pictures that will match the story. The designer hires an artist to draw the pictures. The artist does not talk to the author.

When everything is ready, I send the pictures and story to the printer. The printer and binder put all of the pieces together and ship the finished books to our warehouse. From the warehouse, we ship the books to stores and libraries around the world. I know that you are a writer, too. Does some of the work I do look like the work you do when you write? Maybe someday, you will send me one of your stories.

Emma's Job

1. Put the steps of the publishing process in order from 1–12.

_____ The editor helps the author rewrite the story.

_____ The author gets an idea.

_____ The printer and binder put the book together.

_____ The editor offers to publish the story.

_____ The artist draws the pictures.

_____ The editor plans what the book will look like with the designer.

_____ The author writes a story.

_____ The designer hires an artist.

_____ The author sends the story to the editor.

_____ The books are shipped around the world.

_____ The author rewrites the story until it is just right.

_____ You buy the book in a bookstore.

2. Think about the process you go through when you write. Write the steps you take in your writing process.

_____

_____

_____

3. Which of the steps in your writing process are just like the steps in publishing a book?

_____

_____

_____

Comparing Decimals

When comparing decimals, if more of a portion is shaded, this is the greater number.

0.5 **>** 0.2   0.21 **<** 0.34

Another strategy is to compare the digits in the tenths columns. **0.8 > 0.5** If the digits in the tenths columns are the same, compare the digits in the hundredths columns. **0.63 < 0.69**

Compare the decimals using < or >.

1. 0.6 ◯ 0.4   0.1 ◯ 0.5   0.23 ◯ 0.03   0.6 ◯ 0.9

2. 0.06 ◯ 0.60   0.4 ◯ 0.7   0.9 ◯ 0.5   0.7 ◯ 0.6

3. 0.42 ◯ 0.14   0.72 ◯ 0.27   0.25 ◯ 0.52   0.7 ◯ 0.3

4. 1.4 ◯ 1.6   3.5 ◯ 3.7   16.2 ◯ 16.8   5.21 ◯ 5.38

5. 2.48 ◯ 2.35   14.5 ◯ 14.3   42.6 ◯ 42.3   3.8 ◯ 3.9

6. 0.5 ◯ 0.9   0.4 ◯ 0.26   0.8 ◯ 0.7   0.12 ◯ 0.16

7. 0.1 ◯ 0.01   11.3 ◯ 11.5   0.12 ◯ 2.1   13 ◯ 0.13

8. 0.7 ◯ 0.07   0.6 ◯ 0.4   0.2 ◯ 0.1   0.7 ◯ 0.5

Rounding Decimals

To **round** decimals:
1. Find the place value you want to round to, and look at the digit just to the right of it.
2. If that digit is less than 5, the number you are rounding stays the same.
3. If that digit is greater than or equal to 5, round the number up.

Example: Round to the nearest tenth.

$$421.75 = \mathbf{421.8}$$

You are rounding to this place.

The number to the right tells you whether to round up or down. Since the number is 5, round up.

Study the example above. Then, round to the nearest whole number.

1.	3.67 _____	6.8 _____	11.4 _____	5.9 _____
2.	21.24 _____	10.51 _____	4.9 _____	14.2 _____
3.	8.6 _____	7.8 _____	9.21 _____	10.9 _____
4.	9.7 _____	10.3 _____	8.3 _____	7.4 _____
5.	2.41 _____	12.9 _____	1.02 _____	4.55 _____

Round to the nearest tenth.

6.	6.29 _____	10.68 _____	14.83 _____	6.84 _____
7.	3.48 _____	24.37 _____	17.47 _____	28.15 _____
8.	5.49 _____	10.43 _____	3.56 _____	6.26 _____
9.	17.64 _____	112.26 _____	9.42 _____	400.67 _____
10.	18.25 _____	320.78 _____	62.01 _____	78.45 _____

Tenths

$1\frac{6}{10}$

What portion of this box is shaded?
one whole box

What portion of this box is shaded?
six tenths of the box

Altogether: 1.6 (one and six tenths) Or, "One point six," or "one and six tenths."

$$\frac{1 \cdot 6}{\text{one . six tenths}}$$

Example:

Fraction: $\frac{3}{10}$

Decimal: **0.3**

When there are no whole numbers, place a "0" in the ones place, just to the left of the decimal point.

$$\frac{0 \cdot 3}{\text{no ones . three tenths}}$$

Study the examples above. Then, write as both a fraction and a decimal.

1. Fraction: _____
Decimal: _____

2. Fraction: _____
Decimal: _____

3. Fraction: _____
Decimal: _____

4. Fraction: _____
Decimal: _____

5. Fraction: _____
Decimal: _____

6. Fraction: _____
Decimal: _____

Hundredths

What portion of this box is shaded?
one whole box

What portion of this box is shaded?
five hundredths of a box

Altogether: 1.05 (one and five hundredths)

$\dfrac{1.05}{\text{one . no tenths five hundredths}}$

$1\frac{5}{100}$

Study the examples above. Then, write as both a fraction and a decimal.

1. Fraction: _____
   Decimal: _____

2. Fraction: _____
   Decimal: _____

3. Fraction: _____
   Decimal: _____

4. Fraction: _____
   Decimal: _____

5. Fraction: _____
   Decimal: _____

6. Fraction: _____
   Decimal: _____

7. Fraction: _____
   Decimal: _____

8. Fraction: _____
   Decimal: _____

69

A Day at the Lake

Read the passage.

Erika and Abby rode together in the backseat. They were excited because they were going to the lake. Erika had never been to the lake before. She was going with her best friend Abby and Abby's family.

Abby told Erika all about the sand and the waves. She also told her about the paddleboat. "I like to paddle to the deep part of the lake and jump into the water," said Abby. Erika felt her stomach tighten. She did not know how to swim. She did not know that Abby was so brave in the water. Erika did not say anything.

On the shore of the lake, the girls had a great time. They played in the water. They built a huge sand castle using buckets and shovels. Then, they let water in and created a moat. Erika thought that the lake was great!

Abby's dad called for them to come to the boat dock. He had the paddleboat ready for them and held two life jackets in his hands. Abby ran to the boat, put on her life jacket, and sat down. She smiled and waited for Erika. Erika was very nervous. Abby's dad helped her put on her life jacket. Erika carefully climbed into the seat and put her feet on the pedals. Abby started pedaling, so Erika did, too. Soon, they were moving quickly across the water. Erika was having fun. When they were far out on the lake, Abby stopped the boat and said, "Last one in the lake has stinky feet!" Abby jumped into the water. Erika did not move. She did not dare tell Abby that she could not swim. Would Abby laugh at her?

Abby watched Erika. Finally, she said, "Are you coming in?" When Erika shrugged her shoulders, Abby guessed what was wrong. She climbed back into the boat. "Do you know how to swim yet?" she asked kindly. Erika shook her head. Abby smiled at her friend and said, "OK. Let's paddle around some more. After lunch, I'll teach you a little bit about swimming." Erika smiled at her best friend. Why had she ever worried about telling Abby that she did not know how to swim?

A Day at the Lake

Answer the questions using complete sentences.

1. What do you think Abby would have done if Erika told her earlier that she did not know how to swim?

2. Why do you think Erika waits to tell Abby that she cannot swim?

3. How can Abby tell that Erika does not know how to swim?

4. How do you think Erika can learn how to swim?

5. What do the girls have fun doing at the lake?

6. Do you think that Abby will invite Erika to the lake again? Why or why not?

Circle the words that best describe each girl.

7. What is Erika like?
   - bossy
   - quiet
   - cautious
   - selfish
   - a bad listener
   - a worrier
   - brave
   - nervous
   - unafraid
   - a bad friend

8. What is Abby like?
   - bossy
   - helpful
   - brave
   - caring
   - a bad listener
   - cautious
   - kind
   - nervous
   - selfish
   - a good friend

71

Chris's Adventure

Read the passage.

Chris sat in the chair by the window. The grandfather clock at the bottom of the stairs started to chime. It echoed through the quiet halls.

Chris could hardly keep his eyes open. He knew that his pajamas were laid out neatly on the bed, but he did not want to put them on. If he had to run for help, he wanted to be wearing a shirt, jeans, and sneakers, not flannel pajamas with blue footballs all over them.

When his parents said that he could stay with his uncle while they were in France, he was happy. His other choice was Camp Blue Sky.

Chris hated Camp Blue Sky. At least at his uncle's house, he would have good food, a room of his own, and no leather crafts.

He closed his eyes and counted the clock's strikes—9, 10, 11, 12. He wished that he had chosen Camp Blue Sky. It was not perfect, but it was better than a spooky, old house.

The clock stopped chiming. The house was still. Chris opened his eyes and looked down on the garden. He wanted to see the mysterious light again. If he could tell what it was, he might be able to sleep.

At first, he saw nothing, just dark paths and the reflection of the half moon in a fish pond. Maybe the light that he saw the night before was just a dream.

Suddenly, he saw it again. At first, the white beam flickered. Then, it was steady. It moved across the far side of the garden just beyond the garage. When it came toward the house, Chris dove into bed.

He pulled the covers over his head and waited. His heart pounded. His bedroom door slowly creaked open. He tried to stay still, but he could not help shaking when a voice spoke his name.

Chris's Adventure

Read each pair of sentences. Circle the one that tells what probably happens next.

1. Chris flies to Camp Blue Sky.
   Chris hears his uncle ask, "Are you all right?"

2. Chris pushes the covers back.
   Chris becomes invisible.

3. Chris's uncle says that he went out to the shed to check on the rabbits.
   Chris's uncle turns into a rabbit.

4. Chris's uncle is glowing.
   Chris's uncle has a flashlight.

5. Chris's uncle takes him out to see the rabbits.
   Chris's uncle tells him to clean the room.

6. Chris goes home.
   Chris puts on his pajamas and goes to sleep.

Extra! Write your own ending to the story.

_____

_____

_____

_____

_____

_____

Polygons

When 3 or more line segments come together, they form a **polygon**.

The points where the line segments meet are called **vertices**.

vertices

A polygon with 3 sides: triangle

A polygon with 4 sides: quadrilateral

A polygon with 5 sides: pentagon

Study the examples above. Then, identify each polygon as a triangle, a quadrilateral, or a pentagon.

1. _____ _____ _____ _____

2. _____ _____ _____ _____

3. _____ _____ _____ _____

A **parallelogram** is a special type of quadrilateral that has opposite sides that are parallel and the same length.

parallel

A **rectangle** is a parallelogram that has 4 right angles.

A **square** is a rectangle with 4 sides equal in length.

Identify each polygon as a parallelogram, a rectangle, or a square.

4. _____ _____ _____ _____

74

Similar and Congruent Figures

Figures that are the same shape but not the same size are called **similar**.	Figures that are the same size and shape are called **congruent**.

Study the examples above. Then, using a ruler, connect the dots to draw lines to the figures that are similar. Are the 2 figures you made similar? _____

Using a ruler, connect the dots to draw lines to the figures that are congruent. Are the 2 figures you made congruent? _____

Labeling Congruency and Movements

Congruent means two shapes are exactly the same in size and shape. The congruent figures may look different because their positions are different. The change in direction is called **movement,** and there are 3 types.

slide   flip   turn (rotate)

Study the examples above and on page 75. Then, decide if each set of shapes is congruent. If they are congruent, label the movement. If they are not congruent, write no.

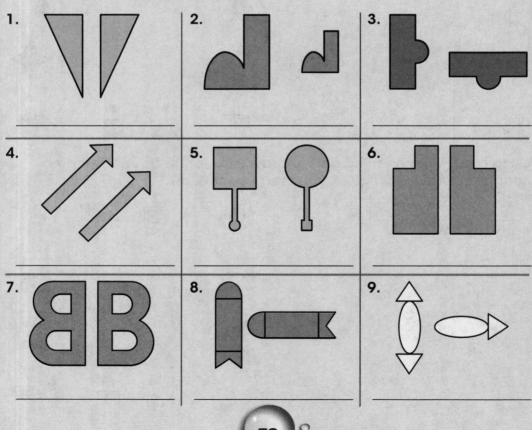

Solid Figures

Solid figures can have many vertices, edges, and faces.

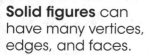

- vertex
- face
- edge

Or, they can have none at all!

cube (6 faces)

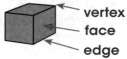

flat face

cone (1 face)

flat face

pyramid (4 or more faces)

flat face

sphere (no faces)

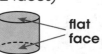

cylinder (2 faces)

flat face

rectangular prism (6 faces)

flat face

Study the solid figures above. Then, identify each solid figure.

1.

_____   _____   _____   _____

2.

_____   _____   _____   _____

3.

_____   _____   _____   _____

4.

_____   _____   _____   _____

The Junior Detectives

Read the passage.

Junior detective Jacob Wilson held a mirror in one hand and a Morse code book in the other. He was trying to figure out how to reflect sunlight with the mirror. He wanted to flash messages to his friend Matthew, who lived in the house across the street. He and Matthew got the idea from a spy movie they saw on television.

Jacob glanced over at Matthew's window. Something flashed. There were long flashes and short flashes. It was a message! Jacob wrote down a dash for each long flash and a dot for each short flash. When the flashing stopped, Jacob looked in his code book. The message was "C-o-m-e q-u-i-c-k."

Jacob climbed down the ladder. He wondered why Matthew wanted him to come over. The two of them did most of their detective club business up in the tree. It was more secret there.

When he knocked on the door to Matthew's room, his friend said, "Password?"

It took Jacob a minute to remember it. "Operation Reflect," he said.

The door opened. "It took you long enough," Matthew said.

Josh, a boy in their class, was sitting on Matthew's bed. Jacob waved to him and then made himself comfortable in the chair by Matthew's computer.

"So, what's going on?" Jacob asked.

"Josh has a new case for us," said Matthew. "It's a secret message. He found it when he got home from school."

Matthew handed Jacob a white pillowcase. The message was printed in pale blue ink. It was a group of strange symbols. It looked like this:

Friday Only: Two Pounds for the Price of One.

"What does it mean?" Jacob asked.

"We've been trying to figure it out for an hour," said Matthew.

Jacob spread the pillowcase out in his lap. He happened to look up and see his reflection in the mirror on Matthew's closet door.

"I have it!" he said.

He held the pillowcase up to the mirror. Matthew and Josh laughed.

"Somebody must have dropped some junk mail in the washing machine again," said Josh.

Hold this page up to a mirror. What does the message say?

_____

_____

The Junior Detectives

Circle the letter next to the best answer for each question.

1. What kind of a clubhouse do Jacob and Matthew have?

A. a cave

B. a tree house

C. a shed

2. What symbols are used in Morse code?

A. long and short dashes

B. red, blue, and yellow beams of light

C. patterns of shapes

3. What does each group of Morse code symbols stand for?

A. a secret place

B. an important person

C. a letter of the alphabet

4. The word *reflection* comes from which of the following words?

A. flecks

B. reveal

C. reflect

5. What must have happened while Josh was at school?

A. Someone washed his pillowcase.

B. His mom went shopping.

C. His dog slept on the bed.

6. What kind of sale is the advertisement announcing?

A. clothes

B. shoes

C. groceries

Extra! Find a Morse code key in an encyclopedia or online. Write a short message in dots and dashes. Trade messages with a friend.

79

The Shortcut

Read the story.

We should have taken the road home from the baseball park. It was getting dark, though, and we decided to take the shortcut home. I was the oldest and should have made a better choice. I did not know that there would be a train.

The shortcut from the baseball park to home was along the railroad tracks. After Reggie's game ended, we were excited. The game had gone into overtime, and Reggie's team had won! As we walked, Reggie and I gave each other high fives. Samantha and Brittany were chewing on their candy necklaces while they ran to keep up. When we came to the turn for the shortcut, we were so excited and happy that we just took it. We should have stayed on the road.

We walked for about five minutes on the tracks. The sides of the tracks were steep, and there were thick bushes and marshy water at the bottom. We stayed on the tracks. Samantha asked how we would know when a train was coming. I said that we would feel the tracks rumbling.

It was then that I heard the train whistle from far away. You can never tell when a train will come through. I did not want to worry the little ones, so I just said as calmly as I could, "Let's go back to the road." We turned around, and I walked pretty fast. Everyone followed.

Soon, we felt the tracks rumbling, and I shouted, "Run!" I grabbed Brittany in my arms, and Reggie held Samantha's hand. We ran as fast as we could. Then, I could see the headlights, and the train blew its loud whistle. We kept running, and I shouted, "Get off the tracks, now!" We jumped off the tracks. We all slid down the sides, trying hard to keep out of the scratchy bushes. Samantha and Brittany were crying, but I could not hear them. The loud train was rushing by us.

After the train went by, we climbed back up the hill. We were all scratched up from the bushes, but no one complained. We were all shaking as we walked back to the road. We did not have to talk. We all knew that we would never take the shortcut home again.

The Shortcut

Answer the following questions.

1. What bad decision do the children make?

_____

_____

2. In what way are the children brave?

_____

_____

3. In what way are the children careless?

_____

_____

4. Do you think that all of the children know that they are in danger when the train whistle blows the first time? _____

Why do you think that?_____

_____

5. Why are the children shaking as they walk back to the road?

_____

_____

6. Do you think that they will ever take the shortcut home again?_____

Why do you think that?_____

_____

Perimeter

The **perimeter (P)** of a figure is the distance around that figure. The perimeter is measured in units, which may be inches, centimeters, miles, etc. To find the perimeter, add all of the sides together.

8 cm

2 cm | | 2 cm

8 cm

8 cm + 2 cm + 8 cm + 2 cm = 20 centimeters

Study the example above. Then, find the perimeter of each figure. Label your answer in the units indicated.

1.
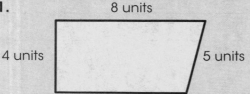
8 units
4 units
5 units
7 units

P = _____

2.
2 units
1 unit
2 units
1 unit
1 unit
3 units

P = _____

3.
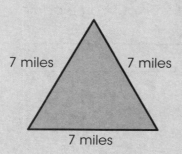
8 inches
10 inches
6 inches

P = _____

4.
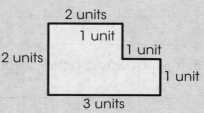
4 cm
4 cm
3 cm
2 cm
2 cm
1 cm

P = _____

5.
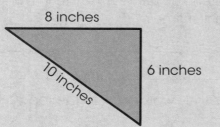
7 miles
7 miles
7 miles

P = _____

6.
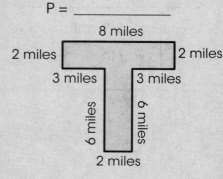
8 miles
2 miles
2 miles
3 miles
3 miles
6 miles
6 miles
2 miles

P = _____

Area

What is the **area** of rectangle A?
Multiply. **5** feet x **30** feet = **150** square feet
What is the area of rectangle B?
Multiply. **8** feet x **10** feet = **80** square feet
How much larger is rectangle A than rectangle B?
Subtract. **150** square feet – **80** square feet = **70 square feet**

5 ft.

A

B

30 ft.

8 ft.

10 ft.

Study the example above. Then, use the picture to answer each question about the Wong family's upstairs.

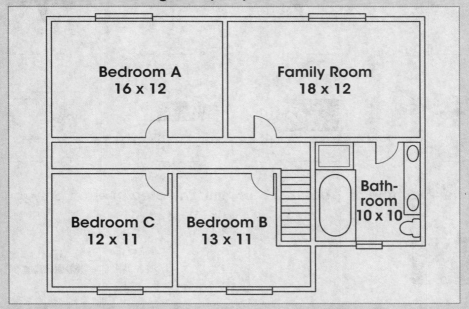

Bedroom A
16 x 12

Family Room
18 x 12

Bedroom C
12 x 11

Bedroom B
13 x 11

**Bath-
room
10 x 10**

1. What is the area of the family room? _____ sq. ft.

2. How much larger is the family room than bedroom C? _____ sq. ft.

3. How many square feet do the 3 bedrooms total? _____ sq. ft.

4. What is the square footage of the bathroom? _____ sq. ft.

5. What is the total square footage of the entire upstairs? _____ sq. ft.

Perimeter and Area Practice

Remember: The perimeter is the distance around an object. Add the sides together to find the perimeter.	**Remember:** The area is the amount of square units within that object. Multiply the 2 sides of the object to find the area.

Study the example on page 82. Then, find the perimeter of each polygon.

1.

P = _____ cm   P = _____ in.   P = _____ m   P = _____ cm

2.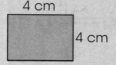

P = _____ in.   P = _____ yd.   P = _____ ft.   P = _____ in.

Study the example on page 83. Then, find the area of each polygon.

3.

4 cm

4 cm

4 yd.

10 yd.

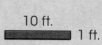
10 ft.
1 ft.

A = _____ sq. cm   A = _____ sq. yd.   A = _____ sq. ft.

4.

10 m

6 m

3 yd.

5 yd.

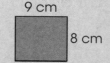
9 cm

8 cm

A = _____ sq. m   A = _____ sq. yd.   A = _____ sq. cm

Volume

You can find the **volume** by counting the cubic units that a figure contains. The volume is written in cubic units.

4 cm x 2 cm x 2 cm = **16 cubic centimeters**

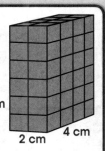

2 cm
2 cm
4 cm

You can also multiply the length by the width by the height (l x w x h = v).
2 cm x 4 cm x 6 cm = **48 cubic centimeters**

6 cm
2 cm   4 cm

Study the examples above. Then, find the volume of each object.

1.

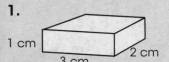
1 cm
3 cm   2 cm

1 m
1 m   1 m

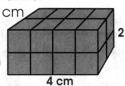
3 in.
3 in.   1 in.

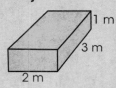
1 m
3 m
2 m

_____ cu. cm   _____ cu. m   _____ cu. in.   _____ cu. m

2.

4 ft.
2 ft.   2 ft.

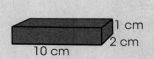
1 cm
2 cm
10 cm

6 ft.
2 ft.   3 ft.

_____ cu. ft.   _____ cu. cm   _____ cu. ft.

What is the total volume of this skyscraper model?

3. level 4 volume = _____ cu. in.

4. level 3 volume = _____ cu. in.

5. level 2 volume = _____ cu. in.

6. level 1 volume = _____ cu. in.

7. total volume = _____ cu. in.

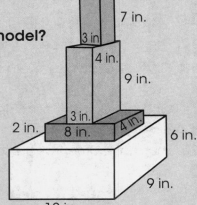

1 in.
7 in.
3 in
4 in.
9 in.
3 in.
2 in.   8 in.   4 in.
6 in.
9 in.
12 in.

Why Did That Happen?

There are times when one thing causes another thing to happen. This is a cause-and-effect relationship. The **cause** is the reason, and the **effect** is the result.

Example: April showers bring May flowers.
"April showers" is the cause. "Bring May flowers" is the effect.

Causes are on the left. Effects are on the right. Write the letter of the effect on the line after its cause.

1. After a week of rain, _____

2. When the car came to a sudden stop, _____

3. My bike hit a rock in the road, _____

4. With a minute left, we scored a goal _____

5. In chemistry class, we mixed the two chemicals and _____

6. After the drive on the dusty dirt roads, _____

7. There was a loud crash outside, _____

8. I heard the bell ring _____

9. When the dog heard the thunder, _____

10. It would soon be dark enough _____

11. We went to the airport _____

12. The team practiced every day _____

13. Once the lawn mower motor started, _____

14. On Saturday, my dad tripped on the doormat _____

15. The mail carrier rang our bell _____

A. and broke his ankle.

B. smoke filled the laboratory.

C. to shoot off fireworks.

D. to win the soccer game 5 to 4.

E. to pick up our guests.

F. the car needed a bath.

G. the river rose over its banks.

H. because he had a special-delivery letter.

I. the seat belt tightened.

J. so I ran to see what happened.

K. and it flew into the air with me still on it.

L. in preparation for the big game.

M. and ran the rest of the way to school.

N. he hid under the bed.

O. Father was able to cut the grass.

Sara's Day

Read each pair of sentences. Write *effect* on the line after each sentence that states an effect. Write *cause* on the line after each sentence that states a cause.

1. Sara watched a scary movie on television. _____
   Sara could not sleep. _____

2. Sara was late for school. _____
   Sara woke up late. _____

3. Sara had to do her homework during recess. _____
   Sara forgot to bring her homework to school. _____

4. Sara left her lunch ticket at home. _____
   Sara had to wait in the lost-ticket line. _____

5. Sara had to answer history questions during P.E. _____
   Sara fell asleep during history class. _____

6. Sara felt better. _____
   On her way home, Sara told a friend about her bad day. _____

7. That night, Sara watched a comedy. _____
   Sara laughed. _____

8. She woke up right on time. _____
   Sara got a good night's sleep. _____

Extra! Read *If You Give a Mouse a Cookie* or *If You Give a Moose a Muffin* by Laura Joffe Numeroff. Look for examples of cause and effect in the story.

87

Beavers

Read the passage.

Beavers are good swimmers. They are at home on land and underwater. They spend their lives around streams. They eat the soft, inner bark of trees and bushes that grow near water. They like to eat aspens, birches, and willows.

Many of the places where beavers live are very cold in the winter. Their dams help them create homes that are safe and comfortable in frigid weather.

Ice forms on top of a beaver pond, but the water underneath does not freeze. Maybe you have heard the saying "busy as a beaver." During the late summer and early fall, beavers are very busy, indeed. They store supplies of branches and sticks underwater. When winter arrives, they do not have to hibernate. They swim out under the ice to get the food that they have saved.

The beaver family builds a home, called a *lodge*, on the bank of a stream or in a shallow part of a pond. The entrance to the lodge is underwater, but the floor is above the waterline. The lodge has a roof made of sticks and branches. It stays dry and cozy all winter.

Read each pair of sentences. Draw a line from the sentence that states the cause to the word *cause*. Draw a line from the sentence that states the effect to the word *effect*.

1. A pond forms behind the dam.   cause
2. A beaver family builds a dam across a stream.   effect

3. Ice forms on top of the pond, but the water   cause
   underneath does not freeze.
4. The pond is deep.   effect

5. The floor of the lodge is above the waterline.   cause
6. The inside of the lodge is warm and dry.   effect

7. The entrance tunnels are underwater.   cause
8. Beavers can swim out under the ice.   effect

Addition and Subtraction

The problems on this page tell a story. Your job is to use information from the story to make a math problem and solve the problem. This is called **problem solving.**

Smoky Joe's Barbecue

MAIN DISHES	SIDE DISHES	BEVERAGES
Eye-Watering Ham.. $3.50	Flame Fries $1.10	Cola $0.75
Burning Hot Ribs $3.75	Sizzlin' Salad $1.05	Lemonade............ $0.85
Rockin' Roast Beef.. $4.25	Poppin' Potatoes . $0.95	Milk $0.95

Study the menu above. Then, solve each problem.

1. Ariel ordered ribs and lemonade. How much will her lunch cost?

2. Michael ordered roast beef. He paid with a 5-dollar bill. How much change will he get?

3. Jonas has $4.08. He buys ham as a main dish. How much money does Jonas have left?

4. Terone wonders, "How much does an order of ribs, fries, and a cola cost?"

5. How much more is roast beef than milk?

6. Traci buys lemonade for herself and 3 friends. How much does she spend?

Multiplication

Some story problems can be answered using multiplication. They ask you to find a total number. This is similar to addition. The difference is that these stories involve equal sets.

Example:

Matthew orders 3 ice cream cones. Each cone has 2 scoops. How many scoops of ice cream did Matthew order?

$$3 \quad \times \quad 2 \quad = \quad 6$$

number of sets   number in each set   total scoops

Study the example above. Then, solve each problem.

1. Gwen's 3 guinea pigs ate 24 seeds each. How many seeds did the guinea pigs eat?

2. We found 6 spider webs. Each web had trapped 17 bugs. How many bugs were trapped?

3. A ticket to the game costs $26.00. Amy wants to invite 4 friends. How much money does Amy need for tickets?

4. Our class ate 9 pizzas. Each pizza had 12 slices. How many slices of pizza did our class eat?

5. We passed 8 trucks on the highway. Each truck honked 4 times. How many honks did the trucks make in all?

6. Haley has 52 dimes in her bank. She has 39 nickels. How many coins does she have?

Division

Some story problems can be answered using division. They ask you to find missing parts or make smaller groups. They involve making equal sets, like these:

Example:

Yasmine had 9 hair ribbons. She split them evenly between 3 girls. How many ribbons did each girl get?

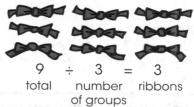

9 ÷ 3 = 3
total   number   ribbons
        of groups

Study the example above. Then, solve each problem.

1. The Millers have 6 children. When they come to the pool, they bring 36 toys that are equally shared. How many toys does each child get?

2. We found 11 flowers. Each one had 8 petals. How many petals does that make?

3. A car travels 120 miles in 3 hours. How many miles per hour does the car travel?

4. Mrs. Weitz passes out 24 papers equally to 8 students. How many papers does each child get?

5. Tara and Lacy share 12 cookies evenly. How many cookies does each girl get?

6. Luke is coloring eggs. Each container holds 12 eggs. Luke has 3 different colors. How many eggs can he color evenly per color?

Choosing the Operation

Look for key words when deciding which operation to use. Here are a few examples of what to look for:

Addition: How many are there **in all, or altogether?**

Subtraction: How many were **left,** or **leftover,** or **remaining?** What is the **difference?**

Multiplication: Look for the total of multiple groups.

Division: Look for the total given and the question asking for how many in each group.

Write which operation you should use in each problem. Solve each problem.

1. Tom volunteered 3 Saturdays this month at the food bank. Ethan volunteered 4. Lenny wants to help others and volunteered 5 times! What is the total number of Saturdays they worked at the food bank?

   Operation: _____
   Answer: _____

2. This week, 27 girls signed up for ballet class. Last week, 16 girls signed up. How many more signed up this week?

   Operation: _____
   Answer: _____

3. A total of 200 students showed up for the bike rodeo on Saturday. Each of the 5 volunteers checked the same number of bikes to make sure they were safe. How many bikes did each volunteer check?

   Operation: _____
   Answer: _____

4. Mr. Bright was dunked 5 times by each of the 3 students that stepped up to see him plunge into the freezing cold water at the carnival! How many times was Mr. Bright dunked in all?

   Operation: _____
   Answer: _____

Page 14: One reason to classify animals is to determine which ones are related to each other.; Monkey and apes belong to a group called *primates*.; Early primates probably ate insects, but they probably also ate leaves and fruits.

Page 15: 1. B.; **2.** A.; **3.** B.; Answers will vary.

Page 16: Insects are truly amazing animals.; Insects do many of the same things that we do, but they do them in unique ways.; Some insects are beneficial to humans.; Some insects are harmful to humans.; Although all insects have six legs, three body parts, and two antennae, each species of insects is unique.

Page 17: 1. B.; **2.** A.

Page 18: 1. 905, 730, 340, 172; **2.** 2,314; 1,170; 800, 512; **3.** 6,000; 4,000; 982, 960; **4.** 490, 472, 436, 401; **5.** 17, 71, 87, 107; **6.** 19, 96, 600, 906; **7.** 1,900; 2,700; 4,350; 7,000; **8.** 200, 620; 2,600; 6,200

Page 19: 1. 9,000 + 500 + 10 + 6; **2.** 2,000 + 300 + 50 + 8; **3.** 1,000 + 400 + 0 + 7; **4.** 900 + 20 + 1; **5.** 7,000 + 800 + 0 + 0; **6.** 3,000 + 200 + 60 + 4; **7.** 5,000 + 100 + 80 + 2; **8.** 600 + 10 + 4; **9.** 4,000 + 0 + 70 + 3; **10.** 9,000 + 500 + 30 + 0

Page 20: 1. >, >, <; **2.** <, >, =; **3.** >, <, >; **4.** >, =, <; **5.** <, >, <; **6.** =, >, >; **7.** >, <; **8.** >, <

Page 21: 1. 70, 10; **2.** 80, 50; **3.** 60, 60; **4.** 20, 30; **5.** 30, 100; **6.** 70, 40; **7.** 300, 600; **8.** 800, 700; **9.** 900, 400; **10.** 700, 200; **11.** 800, 400; **12.** 20,000; 70,000; 600,000; **13.** 4,000; 6,000; 8,000; **14.** 10,000; 4,000; 6,000; **15.** 40,000; 30,000; 6,000,000

Page 22: 1. two rungs; **2.** when Mike was about two years old; **3.** 3; **4.** two weeks; **5.** reading on patio; **6.** animal shelter

Page 23: 1. listen, look left, right, left; **2.** between parked cars, run, walk slowly, doting yellow light; **3.** on crosswalk or at comer; **4.** carry a flashlight and wear bright clothing; **5.** on the left side facing traffic

Page 25: Drawings will vary, but should represent the correct stage of the Saguaro Cactus's life cycle. Labels (clockwise from the top): Seed sprouts, 50 years, animal homes, flowers, fruit, 100 years

Page 26: 1. 93, 86, 133, 97, 132; **2.** 722, 615, 807, 860, 681; **3.** 679; 1,026; 1,166; 1,093; 1,056; **4.** 531, 478, 3, 293, 816; MATH IS A BLAST!

Page 27: Across: 1. 2,535; **2.** 550,450; **3.** 5,350; **4.** 76,472; **5.** 19,290; **6.** 2,400; **7.** 27,305; **8.** 37,496; **Down: 4.** 72,400; **9.** 38,225; **10.** 1,146; **11.** 35,225; **12.** 55,330; **13.** 4,220; **14.** 41,270; **15.** 72,090

Page 28: 1. $1.43, $8.27, $70.61, $0.56; **2.** $0.93, $19.17, $604.07, $573.71; **3.** $361.00, $171.05, $270.42, $377.11; **4.** $42.17, $69.83, $85.10; A NEW BICYCLE!

Page 29: 1. 16, 16; **2.** 9, 6; **3.** 6, 5; **4.** 3, 17; **5.** 15, 7; **6.** 13, 17; **7.** 13, 15; **8.** 12, 17; **9.** 15, 12; **10.** 14, 15; **11.** 16, 5; **12.** 12, 6

Page 30: 1. bough, Answers will vary.; **2.** bored, Answers will vary.; **3.** herd, Answers will vary.; **4.** through, Answers will vary.; **5.** ark, Answers will vary.; **6.** which, Answers will vary.; **7.** way, Answers will vary.; **8.** grate, Answers will vary.

Page 31: 1. park; **2.** pet; **3.** rock; **4.** crack; **5.** stick; **6.** watch

Page 32: 1. circled words: row and soldiers, comparison: the way they stand; **2.** circled words: cars and ants, comparison: cars looked as small as ants; **3.** circled words: clowns and sardines, comparison: tightly packed; **4.** circled words: lapping and slopping, comparison: sound the same;

Page 32 (cont'd): 5. circled words: feet and drums, comparison: rhythmic pounding

Page 33: 1. C.; **2.** A.; **3.** B.; **4.** A.; **5.** B.; **6.** A.; **7.** B.; **8.** A.; **9.** B.

Page 34: 1. 5 + 5 + 5 = 15, 5 x 3 = 15; **2.** 3 + 3 = 6, 3 x 2 = 6; **3.** 2 + 2 + 2 + 2 = 8, 2 x 4 = 8; **4.** 4 + 4 = 8, 4 x 2 = 8; **5.** 3 + 3 + 3 = 9, 3 x 3 = 9; **6.** 4 + 4 + 4 = 12, 4 x 3 = 12; **7.** 2 + 2 + 2 = 6, 2 x 3 = 6; **8.** 5 + 5 = 10, 5 x 2 = 10

Page 35: 1. 188, 189, 640, 126; **2.** 549, 144, 637, 208; **3.** 219, 360, 106, 355; **4.** 368, 189, 728, 164

Page 36: 1. 728; 756; 1,062; 2,684; **2.** 1,500; 4,272; 878; 1,330; **3.** 900; 8,199; 708; 2,223; **4.** 1,488; 814; 1,155; 1,740

Page 37: 1. 7,440; 14,420; 10,136; 17,220; **2.** 12,489; 12,546; 7,955; 26,244; **3.** 16,848; 28,764; 12,705; 9,614

Page 38: 1. trip; **2.** plans; **3.** required; **4.** sprinkling; **5.** pupils; **6.** country; **7.** welcomed; **8.** constructed; **9.** finished; **10.** place

Page 39: 1. downplay, exaggerate; **2.** allow, refuse; **3.** lose, find; **4.** stormy, calm; **5.** answer, question; **6.** tiny, enormous; **7.** tardy, prompt; **8.** relaxed, tense; **9.** trash, treasure; **10.** reduce, increase; Answers will vary.

Page 40: 1. addition; **2.** car; **3.** tropics; **4.** train; **5.** trout; **6.** canyon; **7.** fingers; **8.** safe; **9.** blue; **10.** store; **11.** keys; **12.** squirrel; **13.** cows; **14.** stand; **15.** tornado

Page 41: 1. letter; **2.** strong; **3.** trail; **4.** cow; **5.** swift; **6.** cradle; **7.** wood; **8.** sparrow; **9.** brother; **10.** corn

Page 42: 1. five groups of two circled, 2; **2.** three groups of five circled, 5; **3.** three groups of two circled, 2; **4.** two groups of four circled, 4; **5.** three groups of three circled, 3; **6.** four groups of three circled, 3; **7.** six groups of two circled, 2; **8.** three groups of six circled, 6; **9.** seven groups of two circled, 2

Page 43: 1. 16, 49, 18, 12; **2.** 15, 29, 12, 38; **3.** 14, 18, 24, 17

Page 44: 1. 4 r2, 6 r2, 9 r4, 5 r2; **2.** 3 r2, 8 r2, 7 r5, 9 r2; **3.** 6 r3, 4 r3, 4 r4, 9 r7; **4.** 5 r6, 3 r5, 6 r6, 3 r3

Page 45: 1. 3 r3, 4 r2, 5 r10, 9 r7, 8 r4; **2.** 3 r43, 6 r10, 8 r20, 4 r4, 8 r12; **3.** 4 r26, 5 r9, 1 r80, 7 r20, 5 r10

Page 47: 1. B.; **2.** A.; **3.** C.; The importance of dental floss: to get between teeth where toothbrush cannot reach; Tooth cleaners over the years: crushed bones and shells, salt, baking soda, chalk; Tooth cleaning today: toothbrushes, toothpaste, floss; The invention of the toothbrush: William Addis, bone and bristles

Page 49: 1. First-class passengers ate expensive food, had a menu and ate off of china and crystal. Second-class passengers had four-course meals and ate at tables with pretty plates.; **2.** There were sitting rooms in first class; **3.** In third class, families had cabins and others slept in large rooms with other people. In first and second class, everyone had nice cabins.; **4.** They knew that it was special; 1, 2, 1, 3, 2, 3

Page 50: 1. 30, 10:00, 10:30; **2.** 15, 2:00, 2:15; **3.** 35, 7:00, 7:35; **4.** 55, 9:00, 9:55; **5.** 10, 8:00, 8:10; **6.** 50, 4:00, 4:50; **7.** 5, 10:00, 10:05; **8.** 45, 6:00, 6:45

Page 51: 1. 8:00, 7:40, 11:35, 9:05; **2.** 1:32, 12:45, 6:55, 7:30; **3.** 10:45, 2:30, 3:00, 12:00

Page 52: 1. 1; **2.** 5; **3.** 4; **4.** 2; **5.** 20; **6.** 10; **7.** 10; **8.** 12; **9.** 15; **10.** 20; **11.–14.** Answers will vary.

Page 53: 1. $3.90 **2.** $3.80; **3.** $4.05; **4.** $5.40; **5.** $0.50; **6.** $4.05; **7.** $0.85; **8.** $20.00; **9.** $0.81; **10.** $0.05

Page 54: 1. Fact; **2.** Fact; **3.** Fact; **4.** Fact; **5.** Opinion; **6.** Opinion; **7.** Fact; **8.** Fact; **9.** Opinion; **10.** Fact; **11.** Opinion; **12.** Fact

Page 55: 1. Fact;
2. Opinion; **3.** Fact;
4. Opinion; **5.** Fact;
6. Opinion; **7.** Fact;
8. Fact; **9.** Opinion;
10. Fact

Page 57: 1. B., C.; **2.** G.;
3. C.; **4.** B.; **5.** gum
became popular.;
6.–7. Answers will vary.

Page 58: 1. $\frac{3}{10}, \frac{3}{4}, \frac{9}{14}$;
2. $\frac{5}{6}, \frac{7}{8}, \frac{5}{8}$; **3.** $\frac{7}{10}, \frac{7}{12}, \frac{9}{10}$;
4. $\frac{7}{12}, \frac{4}{5}, \frac{5}{16}$

Page 59: 1. $\frac{1}{4}, \frac{2}{3}, \frac{3}{10}$;
2. $\frac{1}{6}, \frac{1}{4}, \frac{3}{8}$; **3.** $\frac{3}{18}, \frac{1}{12}$, 0;
4. $\frac{1}{4}, \frac{1}{10}, \frac{1}{14}$

Page 60: 1. 5, 2, 5, 5; **2.** 2,
3, 4, 9; **3.** 6, 5, 9, 4; **4.** 9, 14,
8, 2; **5.** 4, 9, 8, 15

Page 61: from left to right
and top to bottom: 0.8
(blue), 0.15 (green), 0.73
(green), 0.36 (green),
0.81 (green), 0.1 (blue),
0.7 (blue), 0.6 (blue), 0.4
(blue), 0.9 (blue)

Page 62: 1. The alarm
did not go off in the Cole
house, and everyone
overslept. Charlie had to
run to catch the school
bus. When Charlie found
a seat and sat down,
he ate the apple that
he had grabbed on his
way out the door. If he
had eaten breakfast at
home, he would have
had a three-mile walk to
school.; **2.** Charlie was
glad to be on the bus,
because today was a
special day at school. It

was Field Day. That meant
the entire school was
divided into teams: red,
white, blue, green, yellow,
and orange. Charlie was
wearing a green shirt
because he was on the
green team.

Page 63: 3, 1, 5, 2, 6, 7, 4,
9, 8; 2, 6, 5, 3, 1, 4

Page 65: 1. 5, 1, 10, 4,
9, 7, 2, 8, 3, 11, 6, 12;
2.–3. Answers will vary.

Page 66: 1. >, <, >, <; **2.** <,
<, >, >; **3.** >, >, <, >; **4.** <, <,
<, <; **5.** >, >, >, <; **6.** <, >, >,
<; **7.** >, <, <, >; **8.** >, >, >, >

Page 67: 1. 4, 7, 11, 6;
2. 21, 11, 5, 14; **3.** 9, 8, 9,
11; **4.** 10, 10, 8, 7; **5.** 2, 13,
1, 5; **6.** 6.3, 10.7, 14.8, 6.8;
7. 3.5, 24.4, 17.5, 28.2;
8. 5.5, 10.4, 3.6, 6.3;
9. 17.6, 112.3, 9.4, 400.7;
10. 18.3, 320.8, 62.0, 78.5

Page 68: 1. $\frac{4}{10}$, 0.4; **2.** $\frac{2}{10}$,
0.2; **3.** $\frac{5}{10}$, 0.5; **4.** $1\frac{4}{10}$, 1.4;
5. $1\frac{1}{10}$, 1.1; **6.** $2\frac{9}{10}$, 2.9

Page 69: 1. $\frac{21}{100}$, 0.21;
2. $\frac{47}{100}$, 0.47; **3.** $\frac{34}{100}$, 0.34;
4. $\frac{69}{100}$, 0.69; **5.** $1\frac{7}{100}$, 1.07;
6. $1\frac{2}{100}$, 1.02; **7.** $2\frac{4}{100}$, 2.04;
8. $\frac{1}{100}$, 0.01

Page 71: 1.–2. Answers
will vary.; **3.** Erika did not
want to jump into the
water.; **4.** Answers will
vary.; **5.** They have fun
building sand castles,

playing in the water,
and pedaling in the
paddleboat.; **6.** Answers
will vary.; **7.** quiet, cautious,
a worrier, nervous;
8. helpful, brave, caring,
kind, a good friend

Page 73: 1. Chris hears
his uncle ask, "Are you all
right?"; **2.** Chris pushes
the covers back.;
3. Chris's uncle says that
he went out to the shed
to check on the rabbits.;
4. Chris's uncle has a
flashlight.; **5.** Chris's uncle
takes him out to see the
rabbits.; **6.** Chris puts on
his pajamas and goes to
sleep.; Stories will vary.

Page 74: 1. quadrilateral,
triangle, triangle,
pentagon; **2.** quadrilateral,
triangle, pentagon,
pentagon; **3.** quadrilateral,
triangle, quadrilateral,
pentagon; **4.** square,
parallelogram, rectangle,
parallelogram

Page 75: yes, yes

Page 76: 1. flip; **2.** no;
3. turn; **4.** slide; **5.** no;
6. flip; **7.** turn; **8.** flip;
9. flip

Page 77: 1. pyramid,
cylinder, sphere, cone;
2. cube, rectangular
prism, pyramid, sphere;
3. cylinder, pyramid,
rectangular prism, cube;
4. cone, cone, sphere,
cone

Page 78: Friday Only: Two
Pounds for the Price of
One.

95

Answer Key

Page 79: 1. B.; **2.** A.; **3.** C.; **4.** C.; **5.** A.; **6.** C.; Answers will vary.

Page 81: 1. They take the shortcut home.; **2.** They stay calm and then jump off the tracks.; **3.** They take the shortcut in the first place, especially with smaller kids.; **4.** Answers will vary.; **5.** They were scared.; **6.** The narrator says so in the story.

Page 82: 1. 24 units; **2.** 10 units; **3.** 24 inches; **4.** 16 cm; **5.** 21 miles; **6.** 32 miles

Page 83: 1. 216; **2.** 84; **3.** 467; **4.** 100; **5.** 783

Page 84: 1. 14, 11, 10, 9; **2.** 12, 16, 18, 19; **3.** 16, 40, 10; **4.** 60, 15, 72

Page 85: 1. 6, 48, 9, 6; **2.** 15, 20, 6; **3.** 21; **4.** 108; **5.** 64; **6.** 648; **7.** 841

Page 86: 1. G.; **2.** I.; **3.** K.; **4.** D.; **5.** B.; **6.** F.; **7.** J.; **8.** M.; **9.** N.; **10.** C.; **11.** E.; **12.** L.; **13.** O.; **14.** A.; **15.** H.

Page 87: 1. cause, effect; **2.** effect, cause; **3.** effect, cause; **4.** cause, effect; **5.** effect, cause; **6.** effect, cause; **7.** cause, effect; **8.** effect, cause

Page 88: 1. effect; **2.** cause; **3.** effect; **4.** cause; **5.** cause; **6.** effect; **7.** cause; **8.** effect

Page 89: 1. $3.75 + $0.85 = $4.60; **2.** $5.00 – $4.25 = $0.75; **3.** $4.08 – $3.50 = $0.58; **4.** $3.75 + $1.10 + $0.75 = $5.60; **5.** $4.25 – $0.95 = $3.30; **6.** $0.85 + $0.85 + $0.85 + $0.85 = $3.40

Page 90: 1. 3 x 24 = 72 seeds; **2.** 6 x 17 = 102 bugs; **3.** $26.00 x 5 = $130.00; **4.** 9 x 12 = 108 slices; **5.** 8 x 4 = 32 honks; **6.** 52 + 39 = 91 coins

Page 91: 1. 36 ÷ 6 = 6 toys; **2.** 11 x 8 = 88 petals; **3.** 120 ÷ 3 = 40 miles; **4.** 24 ÷ 8 = 3 papers; **5.** 12 ÷ 2 = 6 cookies; **6.** 12 x 4 = 48 eggs

Page 92: 1. addition, 3 + 4 + 5 = 12 Saturdays; **2.** subtraction, 27 – 16 = 11 girls; **3.** division, 200 ÷ 5 = 40 bikes; **4.** multiplication, 5 x 3 = 15 times